C000195721

D.H. Lawrence (1885–1930), ... ter, critic, is an icon of twentie... writing at an early age, publishir... *cock*, when he was twenty-five, ... and *The Rainbow* and *Women* ... tred of militarism, openly expressed during the ... ... stirred a wave of vilification that forced him to leave England and embark on what he called his 'Savage Pilgrimage'. He spent the remainder of his life travelling – to Italy, Sri Lanka (then called Ceylon), Australia, America, Mexico and the South of France – and it was during this time that he wrote such classics as *Sea and Sardinia, The Plumed Serpent* and *Lady Chatterley's Lover*. With the exception of E. M. Forster, who called him 'the greatest imaginative novelist of our generation', and friends such as Aldous Huxley, Lawrence's obituarists were dismissive and hostile. It was not until The Lady Chatterley Trial thirty years after his death and the subsequent publication of the book that Lawrence was finally recognised as one of the great writers and thinkers of his age.

Michael Squires is the author or editor of nine books on D.H. Lawrence. His most recent, a biography called *D.H. Lawrence and Frieda: A Portrait of Love and Loyalty*, combines a highly readable style with cutting-edge research. *Publishers Weekly* calls it 'fresh and illuminating'. Praising its intimacy, Dermot Bolger calls it 'a short but fascinating account of the years that Lawrence and Frieda spent together'. Squires has also edited *Lady Chatterley's Lover*, Lawrence's most famous novel.

'He wrote something like three dozen books, of which even the worst page dances with life that could be mistaken for no other man's, while the best are admitted, even by those who hate him, to be unsurpassed.'　　　　Catherine Carswell, *Time and Tide*

'He is an extraordinarily acute noticer of the world, human and natural. And it is not just the natural world that beckons Lawrence to flood it with beautiful language . . . he can be as precise and compact an observer of human interaction as Flaubert or Forster.'　　　　James Wood, *Guardian*

Tauris Parke Paperbacks is an imprint of I.B.Tauris. It is dedicated to publishing books in accessible paperback editions for the serious general reader within a wide range of categories, including biography, history, travel and the ancient world. The list includes select, critically acclaimed works of top quality writing by distinguished authors that continue to challenge, to inform and to inspire. These are books that possess those subtle but intrinsic elements that mark them out as something exceptional.

The Colophon of Tauris Parke Paperbacks is a representation of the ancient Egyptian ibis, sacred to the god Thoth, who was himself often depicted in the form of this most elegant of birds. Thoth was credited in antiquity as the scribe of the ancient Egyptian gods and as the inventor of writing and was associated with many aspects of wisdom and learning.

ETRUSCAN PLACES

Travels through Forgotten Italy

D.H. Lawrence

TAURIS PARKE
Bloomsbury Publishing Plc
50 Bedford Square, London, WC1B 3DP, UK
1385 Broadway, 5th Floor, New York, NY 10018

BLOOMSBURY, TAURIS PARKE and the TAURIS PARKE logo are trademarks of
Bloomsbury Publishing Plc

First published in 1932 in London by Martin Secker
Revised paperback edition published in 2011 in Great Britain by Tauris Parke Paperbacks, an
imprint of I.B.Tauris & Co. Ltd

A catalogue record for this book is available from the British Library

Library of Congress Cataloguing-in-Publication data has been applied for

Cover image: Musician playing the Pipes, from the Tomb of the Leopard, c. 490 BC (wall
painting) by Etruscan artist (fifth century BC), Tarquinia, Lazio, Italy © Giraudon / The
Bridgeman Art Library

ISBN: PB: 978-1-83860-022-8; eBook: 978-0-85771-982-9

2 4 6 8 10 9 7 5 3 1

Printed by CPI Group (UK) Ltd, Croydon CR0 4YY

To find out more about our authors and books visit www.bloomsbury.com and sign up for our
newsletters

CONTENTS

CONTENTS

LIST OF ILLUSTRATIONS

READERS today are mostly unaware of D. H. Lawrence's reputation for bold, unconventional writing that
gauges his characters' depths of feeling. In 1913, when he published *Sons and Lovers*, his narrative voice was brash, erotic,
and critical of conservative British norms. In the years that
followed, he wrote tender, tumultuous love stories in passionate prose to celebrate his love for his wife Frieda von
Richthofen. Using their meager savings, the Lawrences left
Europe in 1922 and went by ship around the world. They
tried living in Ceylon, Australia, Mexico, and the United
States, but their deep roots finally called them back to
Europe, where Frieda had grown up in Germany, Lawrence
in England. They were ready to start afresh, though in
Mexico Lawrence had grown ill with malaria and tuberculo-
sis, had never fully recovered, and now guarded his health.
Yet one group of people still appealed to him – the early
Etruscans.

In 1926, Lawrence, now aged 40 years, wrote to a friend,
'I'm reading about the Etruscans, and looking at their remains. They interest me.'[1] Their remains, he thought, showed
the strength of Italy, alive with 'a powerful physicality which
surely is as great, or sacred, ultimately, as the *ideal* of the
Greeks and Germans.'[2] After his stint of world travel had

I

ended, Lawrence moved to Italy, the European country he liked best. There, he wrote, 'the flow of life seems rich and easy.'[3] Frieda agreed: 'I appreciate Tuscany's otherness and delicacy very much,' she added.[4] The Lawrences liked the flowery sunlit days, the slow rural rhythms of peasants tending grapes and olives, and the earthy vigour of the Italians – and stayed from 1925 to 1928.

The ancient Etruscans had settled in Italy around 900 BC, but within 600 years, their civilisation had been absorbed by the Romans. Lawrence had long admired their vases decorated with lively forms, their bronzes, and their fine sculptures; and if he could see their tombs for himself, he might write a volume half of travel, half of history. In his earlier works – in *Sea and Sardinia* (1921) and *Mornings in Mexico* (composed 1924–25) – he had already tried to penetrate another culture in order to illuminate the mysteries that had been concealed from him. His travels had indeed revealed worlds very different from those of Europe, where the Lawrences had lived most of their married life.[5] They had seen the dark-skinned natives of Ceylon, heard the ocean's roar in Australia, stood before the pristine mountains of New Mexico, watched the Indians dance in Arizona, and stared at gun-wielding soldiers in Mexico. In all these places Lawrence had sought 'new gods' (his words)[6] to rescue him from disappointment and ennui. In Mexico and the United States, the Indians had awakened him, yet their silent hostility had kept him just outside the pale of their culture and its empowering mysteries.

In September 1925, when Lawrence and Frieda left their ranch in America to return to Italy, he had not yet discovered the culture that exemplified his ideal. It was an ideal of living in a society that valued not money or power but self-expression grounded in shared community standards which allowed men and women to appreciate physical beauty and to pursue spiritual wisdom. In the essays of *Mornings in Mexico*, he had discovered how much he liked sketching the essence of a foreign place like Mexico, finding its center, and claiming its distinction. But now money was scarce. His British publisher Martin Secker, though loyal, had never paid well, and his American publisher Thomas Seltzer had slid into bankruptcy. In December, Lawrence had railed, 'Why does everything cost, and nothing pay?'[7] Still, travel magazines *would* pay for intriguing articles and might therefore enable him to explore the ancient Etruscans.

After trying Spotorno on the Mediterranean coast, Lawrence and Frieda settled near Florence, renting in May 1926 an old villa outside the city. They picnicked on its sunny slopes and made friends with the peasants. In time Lawrence recognised that the 'new gods' he sought could be found not in living persons but in his imagination and perhaps in his proposed walking trip through central Italy. Now he felt inspired. Between October 1926 and February 1928 he completed a pair of masterful works. He wrote his final novel *Lady Chatterley's Lover* in three versions, and he composed *Etruscan Places*, published in 1932, two years after his death. These two works, arising from the same impulse, share several themes: they aim to celebrate the physical body, full of life; to find beauty in the grip of death; and to reorient the human spirit within the vast cosmos.

The Six Essays

Part of a longer volume that Lawrence did not live to complete, the six essays of *Etruscan Places* capture Lawrence's vivid first-hand experience of seeing the Etruscan tombs and his boldly original assessment of Etruscan values. The essays are spirited, conversational, and adversarial. Each risks strong opinions. Lawrence demanded some form of vital, immediate contact with the Etruscans and their remains. 'The Etruscans,' he groused in his essay on Volterra, 'are not a theory or a thesis. If they are anything, they are an *experience*' (197). He would approach them by feel, using his intuition, and allow their artifacts to speak directly to his sensibility. Having read the scholarly tomes by Etruscan historians such as George Dennis – and found them short on fact and substance – he concluded that in his own book he would 'take the imaginative line.'[8] That meant doing what he did best – weaving a tapestry about ancient life from the threads he found in the sites and museums of the Etruscans. While weaving his tapestry, he would refresh his opposition to his own contemporary culture, whose values he hoped to subvert. By nature he was defiant.

Field work followed. Though often tired, Lawrence had browsed through museums such as the Museo Archeologico in Florence, but he had not descended into the Etruscan tombs (mostly looted or poorly preserved) or considered the long walks and steep climbs that would be required. In the winter his neighbours, the Arthur Wilkinsons, had found him 'very cross' and observed that he '[did]n't look very well.'[9] Nonetheless, determined to go forward, he reached Rome

4

in April 1927. To accompany him on his mission, he asked Earl Brewster (1878–1957), a lanky American painter he had met several years earlier. Brewster possessed a keen intellect, a philosophic calm, and a gift of unselfish friendship. He met Lawrence's irritability with tolerance and sympathy, and drew out Lawrence's compassion as no one else did.

The two friends met in Rome, then travelled north to Cerveteri, Tarquinia, Vulci, and Volterra – sites of Etruscan antiquity. In Cerveteri, beautifully carvèd phallic stones, placed at the tomb entrances, surprised them both. The conspicuous 'double cone' (30) of the male's uncircumcised organ reminded them that the Etruscans' worship of the phallus (and the womb) likely explained why the Romans, fixated on acquiring power, would obliterate the more-sexual Etruscan consciousness. In Cerveteri, finding that the tombs' treasures had been sent to museums, Lawrence and Brewster travelled on to Tarquinia, near the coast, where many tombs had been preserved. There, the urns and vases showed bold but sensitive designs, allowing Lawrence to differentiate what he saw from what he had learned, and to conclude:

> It is useless to look in Etruscan things for 'uplift' [i.e. conventional elegance]. If you want uplift, go to the Greek and the Gothic. If you want mass, go to the Roman. But if you love the odd spontaneous forms that are never to be standardized, go to the Etruscans. (62)

He delighted in the 'spontaneous forms' of simplicity, vitality, and beauty. Guided through the painted tombs of Tarquinia by the light of an acetelyne torch, he soon noticed the sprightly figures of spotted deer, muscled lions, flute players, dancers, naked horsemen, and women with garlands. The Etruscan dancers, for instance, leap and play, revealing what Lawrence had been longing to find: 'They know the gods in their very finger-tips' (85). They live – he explains – to the full depth of their capacity, secure in knowing their place in the cosmos.

In assessing the painted tombs of Tarquinia, Lawrence gradually shapes his quick, personal impressions into a philosophy, but surrounds it with a necklace of judgements comparing ancients and moderns. He arrives at an explanation – what he calls a 'divination' – for the dualities that the tombs reveal. All his life he had practiced such divination: he had prodded his 'religious concentration' till it yielded an 'answer' to whatever was unstable in his mind. This concentration (he understood) was like prayer, visionary insight, or scientific research. Out of it, out of such 'pure attention' (97–98), he now uncovers a mystery previously unrevealed – that the divine cosmos embraces an equilibrium of forces. One force is watery, the other fiery; one is imaged as a swollen udder, the other as a dangerously powerful horn. And so, inside the tombs, the muscled lion attacks the spotted deer, restoring balance. In this way, Lawrence concludes, 'the symbolism goes all through the Etruscan tombs.' (101) In these symbols he locates the crux of the universe – the balance of male and female, darkness and light, fixity and rotation, violence and tenderness.

Not all the essays carry such philosophical weight. On the road again, Lawrence and Brewster reached Vulci on 9 April 1927, where the once-fertile landscape had, in 2000 years, become a *maremma* – a marshland with malaria. The travellers welcomed help in finding the looted, crumbling tombs.

FOREWORD

Lawrence's essay on Vulci, more satirical than the others, follows the two pilgrims and three guides as they descend, groping and wriggling, into gloomy holes, like wolves' dens, to see huge stone coffins strewn amid shattered vases and rubble – and to see, clinging to the roofs, clusters of furry, torpid, pale-brown bats, stupefied by their visitors. The expedition tries Lawrence's courage and goodwill, but his probing questions reveal the modern Italian sensibility as the inverse of Etruscan valor. Modern Italy is only a shadow of Lawrence's dream of Etruscan grace and glamour.

The six essays of *Etruscan Places*, four of which were published as magazine articles, are less coherent as a group than other collections that Lawrence published. Yet all share his adventure in interpreting a culture which, though it endured for only 600 years, touches us still today. With poetic passion, Lawrence meditates on the admirable integrity of the Etruscans, whose dualistic motifs clarify their religion, then asks what, over time, we have lost. The answer is that we have lost the Etruscans' physical delight in food and dance and sex as a platform for knowing the invisible world beyond. By 1926–27, when Lawrence wrote these essays, he had lost confidence in his own civilisation to provide spiritual nourishment, but he had also gained compensatory insights. One is that the cosmos is defined by principles that require a human participation that we have lost. Another is that spiritual equilibrium does not result from energy and force but from freedom to find an empowering balance of oppositions to express our sexual, emotional, and intellectual selves. The Etruscans were physically alive and spiritually triumphant. It is their lively vigour that Lawrence captures. By turns his prose is sprightly, sardonic, wistful, and pungent. His essays show a vividness and a veracity rarely matched. They take readers on a remarkable journey – to pry off the layers of Greek and Roman order, and so reveal the mysterious vitality that Lawrence regarded as profoundly human.

Notes

1. *Letters of D.H. Lawrence*, 8 volumes, various editors (Cambridge University Press, 1979–2000), vol. v, p. 456; DHL to Earl Brewster, 17 May 1926. In the notes that follow, Lawrence's letters are cited as *DHL Letters* by volume and page number.
2. *DHL Letters*, vol. v, pp. 564–65; DHL to Else Jaffe, 26 May 1926.
3. *DHL Letters*, vol. v, p. 467; DHL to Rachel Hawk, 29 May 1926.
4. Frieda Lawrence to Mabel Dodge Luhan, [May 1926], qtd. in Luhan, *Lorenzo in Taos* (New York: Knopf, 1932), p. 307.
5. For a full account of the Lawrences' marriage, see Michael Squires, *D.H. Lawrence and Frieda: A Portrait of Love and Loyalty* (London: André Deutsch, 2008).
6. *DHL Letters*, vol. iv, p. 154; DHL to Earl Brewster, 2 Jan. 1922.
7. *DHL Letters*, vol. v, p. 364; DHL to Dorothy Brett, 29 Dec. 1925.
8. *DHL Letters*, vol. v, p. 473; DHL to Millicent Beveridge, 8 June 1926.
9. Qtd. in John Turner, ed., "D.H. Lawrence in the Wilkinson Diaries," *D.H. Lawrence Review* 30 (2002): 60. Diary entry of 3 Feb. 1927.

A Note on the Text

Etruscan Places by D.H. Lawrence was first published in 1932 by Martin Secker in England and by Viking in America. The text reprinted here is that of the Secker edition.

I
CERVETERI

I

THE Etruscans, as everyone knows, were the people who occupied the middle of Italy in early Roman days, and whom the Romans, in their usual neighbourly fashion, wiped out entirely in order to make room for Rome with a very big R. They couldn't have wiped them all out, there were too many of them. But they did wipe out the Etruscan existence as a nation and a people. However, this seems to be the inevitable result of expansion with a big E, which is the sole *raison d'être* of people like the Romans.

Now, we know nothing about the Etruscans except what we find in their tombs. There are references to them in Latin writers. But of first-hand knowledge we have nothing except what the tombs offer.

So to the tombs we must go: or to the museums containing the things that have been rifled from the tombs.

Myself, the first time I consciously saw Etruscan things, in the museum at Perugia, I was instinctively attracted to them. And it seems to be that way. Either there is instant sympathy, or instant contempt and indifference. Most people despise everything B.C. that isn't Greek, for the good reason that it ought to be Greek if it isn't. So Etruscan things are put down as a feeble Græco-Roman imitation. And a great scientific historian like Mommsen hardly allows that the Etruscans existed at all. Their existence was antipathetic to him. The Prussian in him was enthralled by the Prussian in the all-conquering Romans. So being a great scientific historian, he almost denies the very existence of the Etruscan people. He didn't like the idea of them. That was enough for a great scientific historian.

Besides, the Etruscans were vicious. We know it, because their enemies and exterminators said so. Just as we knew the unspeakable depths of *our* enemies in the late war. Who isn't vicious to his enemy? To my detractors I am a very effigy of vice. *À la bonne heure!*

However, those pure, clean-living, sweet-souled Romans, who smashed nation after nation and crushed the free soul in people after people, and were ruled by Messalina and Heliogabalus and such-like snowdrops, they said the Etruscans were vicious. So *basta! Quand le maître parle, tout le monde se tait.* The Etruscans were vicious! The only vicious people on the face of the earth presumably. You and I, dear reader, we are two unsullied snowflakes, aren't we? We have every right to judge.

Myself, however, if the Etruscans were vicious, I'm glad they were. To the Puritan all things are impure, as somebody says. And those naughty neighbours of the Romans at least escaped being Puritans.

But to the tombs, to the tombs! On a sunny April

morning we set out for the tombs. From Rome, the eternal city, now in a black bonnet. It was not far to go—about twenty miles over the Campagna towards the sea, on the line to Pisa.

The Campagna, with its great green spread of growing wheat, is almost human again. But still there are damp empty tracts, where now the little narcissus stands in clumps, or covers whole fields. And there are places green and foam-white, all with camomile, on a sunny morning in early April.

We are going to Cerveteri, which was the ancient Caere, or Cere, and which had a Greek name too, Agylla. It was a gay and gaudy Etruscan city when Rome put up her first few hovels : probably. Anyhow, there are tombs there now.

The inestimable big Italian railway-guide says the station is Palo, and that Cerveteri is eight and a half kilometres away : about five miles. But there is a post-omnibus.

We arrive at Palo, a station in nowhere, and ask if there is a bus to Cerveteri. No ! An ancient sort of wagon with an ancient white horse stands outside. Where does that go? To Ladispoli. We know we don't want to go to Ladispoli, so we stare at the landscape. Could we get a carriage of any sort? It would be difficult. That is what they always say : difficult ! Meaning impossible. At least they won't lift a finger to help. Is there an hotel at Cerveteri? They don't know. They have none of them ever been, though it is only five miles away, and there are tombs. Well, we will leave our two bags at the station. But they cannot accept them. Because they are not locked. But when did a hold-all ever lock? Difficult! Well then, let us leave them, and steal if you want to. Impossible! Such a moral responsibility! Impossible to leave an unlocked small hold-all at the station. So much for the officials!

However, we try the man at the small buffet. He is very laconic, but seems all right. We abandon our things in a corner of the dark little eating-place, and set off on foot. Luckily it is only something after ten in the morning.

A flat, white road with a rather noble avenue of umbrella-pines for the first few hundred yards. A road not far from the sea, a bare, flattish, hot white road with nothing but a tilted oxen-wagon in the distance like a huge snail with four horns. Beside the road the tall asphodel is letting off its spasmodic pink sparks, rather at random, and smelling of cats. Away to the left is the sea, beyond the flat green wheat, the Mediterranean glistening flat and deadish, as it does on the low shores. Ahead are hills, and a ragged bit of a grey village with an ugly big grey building: that is Cerveteri. We trudge on along the dull road. After all, it is only five miles and a bit.

We creep nearer, and climb the ascent. Caere, like most Etruscan cities, lay on the crown of a hill with cliff-like escarpments. Not that this Cerveteri is an

Etruscan city. Caere, the Etruscan city, was swallowed
by the Romans, and after the fall of the Roman Empire
it fell out of existence altogether. But it feebly revived,
and to-day we come to an old Italian village, walled
in with grey walls, and having a few new, pink, box-
shaped houses and villas outside the walls.

We pass through the gateway, where men are loung-
ing talking and mules are tied up, and in the bits of
crooked grey streets look for a place where we can eat.
We see the notice, *Vini e Cucina*, Wines and Kitchen;
but it is only a deep cavern where mule-drivers are
drinking blackish wine.

However, we ask the man who is cleaning the post-
omnibus in the street if there is any other place. He
says no, so in we go, into the cavern, down a few steps.

Everybody is perfectly friendly. But the food is as
usual, meat broth, very weak, with thin macaroni in
it: the boiled meat that made the broth: and tripe:
also spinach. The broth tastes of nothing, the meat
tastes almost of less, the spinach, alas! has been cooked
over in the fat skimmed from the boiled beef. It is a
meal—with a piece of so-called sheep's cheese, that is
pure salt and rancidity, and probably comes from
Sardinia; and wine that tastes like, and probably is,
the black wine of Calabria wetted with a good proportion of water. But it is a meal. We will go to the
tombs.

Into the cavern swaggers a spurred shepherd wearing goatskin trousers with the long, rusty brown goat's

hair hanging shaggy from his legs. He grins and
drinks wine, and immediately one sees again the
shaggy-legged faun. His face is a faun-face, not
deadened by morals. He grins quietly, and talks very
subduedly, shyly, to the fellow who draws the wine
from the barrels. It is obvious fauns are shy, very shy,
especially of moderns like ourselves. He glances at us
from a corner of his eye, ducks, wipes his mouth on
the back of his hand, and is gone, clambering with his
hairy legs on to his lean pony, swirling, and rattling
away with a neat little clatter of hoofs, under the
ramparts and away to the open. He is the faun escap-
ing again out of the city precincts, far more shy and
evanescent than any Christian virgin. You cannot
hard-boil him.

It occurs to me how rarely one sees the faun-face
now, in Italy, that one used to see so often before the
war: the brown, rather still, straight-nosed face with
a little black moustache and often a little tuft of black
beard; yellow eyes, rather shy under long lashes, but
able to glare with a queer glare, on occasion; and
mobile lips that had a queer way of showing the teeth
when talking, bright white teeth. It was an old, old
type, and rather common in the South. But now
you will hardly see one of these men left, with the
unconscious, ungrimacing faun-face. They were all,
apparently, killed in the war: they would be sure not
to survive such a war. Anyway the last one I know,
a handsome fellow of my own age—forty and a bit—

is going queer and morose, crushed between war memories, that have revived, and remorseless go-ahead womenfolk. Probably when I go South again he will have disappeared. They can't survive, the faun-faced men, with their pure outlines and their strange non-moral calm. Only the deflowered faces survive.

So much for a Maremma shepherd! We went out into the sunny April street of this Cerveteri, Cerevetus, the old Caere. It is a worn-out little knot of streets shut in inside a wall. Rising on the left is the citadel, the acropolis, the high place, that which is the arx in Etruscan cities. But now the high place is forlorn, with a big, weary building like a governor's palace, or a bishop's palace, spreading on the crest behind the castle gate, and a desolate sort of yard tilting below it, surrounded by ragged, ruinous enclosure. It is forlorn beyond words, dead, and still too big for the grey knot of inhabited streets below.

The girl of the cavern, a nice girl but a bad cook, has found us a guide, obviously her brother, to take us to the necropolis. He is a lad of about fourteen, and like everybody in this abandoned place shy and suspicious, holding off. He bids us wait while he runs away somewhere. So we drink coffee in the tiny café outside which the motor-omnibus reposes all day long, till the return of our guide and another little boy, who will come with him and see him through. The two boys cotton together, make a little world secure from us, and move on ahead of us, ignoring us as far as possible. The stranger is always a menace. B. and I are two very quiet-mannered harmless men. But that first boy could not have borne to go alone with us. Not alone! He would have been afraid, as if he were in the dark.

They led us out of the only gate of the old town. Mules and ponies were tied up in the sloping, forlorn place outside, and pack-mules arrived, as in Mexico. We turned away to the left, under the rock cliff from whose summit the so-called palace goes up flush, the windows looking out on to the world. It seems as if the Etruscans may once have cut this low rock-face, and as if the whole crown on which the wall-girt village of Cerveteri now stands may once have been the arx, the ark, the inner citadel and holy place of the city of Caere, or Agylla, the splendid Etruscan city, with its Greek quarters. There was a whole suburb of Greek colonists, from Ionia, or perhaps from Athens, in busy Caere when Rome was still a rather crude place. About the year 390 B.C. the Gauls came swooping down on Rome. Then the Romans hurried the Vestal Virgins and other women and children away to Caere, and the Etruscans took care of them, in their rich city. Perhaps the refugee Vestals were housed on this rock. And perhaps not. The site of Caere may not have been exactly here. Certainly it stretched away on this same hilltop, east and south, occupying the whole of the small plateau, some four or five miles round, and spreading a great city thirty times as big as the present

Cerveteri. But the Etruscans built everything of wood—houses, temples—all save walls for fortification, great gates, bridges, and drainage works. So that the Etruscan cities vanished as completely as flowers. Only the tombs, the bulbs, were underground. But the Etruscans built their cities, whenever possible, on a long narrow plateau or headland above the surrounding country, and they liked to have a rocky cliff for their base, as in Cerveteri. Round the summit of this cliff, this headland, went the enclosure wall, sometimes miles of the great cincture. And within the walls they liked to have one inner high place, the arx, the citadel. Then outside they liked to have a sharp dip or ravine, with a parallel hill opposite. And on the parallel hill opposite they liked to have their city of the dead, the necropolis. So they could stand on their ramparts and look over the hollow where the stream flowed among its bushes, across from the city of life, gay with its painted houses and temples, to the near-at-hand city of their dear dead, pleasant with its smooth walks and stone symbols, and painted fronts.

So it is at Cerveteri. From the sea-plain—and the sea was probably a mile or two miles nearer in, in Etruscan days—the land leaves the coast in an easy slope to the low-crowned cliffs of the city. But behind, turning out of the gate away from the sea, you pass under the low but sheer cliff of the town, down the stony road to the little ravine, full of bushes.

Down here in the gully, the town—village, rather—

has built its wash-house, and the women are quietly washing the linen. They are good-looking women, of the old world, with that very attractive look of noise-lessness and inwardness, which women must have had in the past. As if, within the woman, there were again something to seek, that the eye can never search out. Something that can be lost, but can never be found out.

Up the other side of the ravine is a steep, rocky little climb along a sharp path, the two lads scrambling subduedly ahead. We pass a door cut in the rock-face. I peep in to the damp, dark cell of what was apparently once a tomb. But this must have been for unimportant people, a little room in a cliff-face, now all deserted. The great tombs in the Banditaccia are covered with mounds, tumuli. No one looks at these damp little rooms in the low cliff-face, among the bushes. So I scramble on hastily, after the others.

To emerge on to the open, rough, uncultivated plain. It was like Mexico, on a small scale: the open, abandoned plain; in the distance little, pyramid-shaped mountains set down straight upon the level, in the not-far distance; and between, a mounted shepherd galloping round a flock of mixed sheep and goats, looking very small. It was just like Mexico, only much smaller and more human.

The boys went ahead across the fallow land, where there were many flowers, tiny purple verbena, tiny forget-me-nots, and much wild mignonette, that had a sweet little scent. I asked the boys what they called it. They gave the usual dumb-bell answer: "It is a flower!" On the heaping banks towards the edge of the ravine the asphodel grew wild and thick, with tall flowers up to my shoulder, pink and rather spasmodic. These asphodels are very noticeable, a great feature in all this coast landscape. I thought the boys surely would have a name for it. But no! Sheepishly they make the same answer: "*È un fiore! Puzza!*"—It is a flower. It stinks!—Both facts being self-evident, there was no contradicting it. Though the smell of the asphodel is not objectionable, to me: and I find the flower, now I know it well, very beautiful, with its way of opening some pale, big, starry pink flowers, and leaving many of its buds shut, with their dark, reddish stripes.

Many people, however, are very disappointed with the Greeks, for having made so much of this flower. It is true, the word "asphodel" makes one expect some tall and mysterious lily, not this sparky, assertive flower with just a touch of the onion about it. But for me, I don't care for mysterious lilies, not even for that weird shyness the mariposa lily has. And having stood on the rocks in Sicily, with the pink asphodel proudly sticking up like clouds at sea, taller than myself, letting off pink different flowerets with such sharp and vivid éclat, and saving up such a store of buds in ear, stripey, I confess I admire the flower. It has a certain reckless glory, such as the Greeks loved.

One man said he thought we were mistaken in calling this the Greek asphodel, as somewhere in Greek the asphodel is called yellow. Therefore, said this scholastic Englishman, the asphodel of the Greeks was probably the single daffodil.

But not it! There is a very nice and silky yellow asphodel on Etna, pure gold. And heaven knows how common the wild daffodil is in Greece. It does not seem a very Mediterranean flower. The narcissus, the polyanthus narcissus, is pure Mediterranean, and Greek. But the daffodil, the Lent lily!

However, trust an Englishman and a modern for wanting to turn the tall, proud, sparky, dare-devil asphodel into the modest daffodil! I believe we don't like the asphodel because we don't like anything proud and sparky. The myrtle opens her blossoms in just the same way as the asphodel, explosively, throwing out the sparks of her stamens. And I believe it was just this that the Greeks *saw*. They were that way themselves.

However, this is all on the way to the tombs: which lie ahead, mushroom-shaped mounds of grass, great mushroom-shaped mounds, along the edge of the ravine. When I say ravine, don't expect a sort of Grand Canyon. Just a modest, Italian sort of ravine-gully, that you could almost jump down.

When we come near we see the mounds have bases of stone masonry, great girdles of carved and bevelled stone, running round touching the earth in flexible, uneven lines, like the girdles on big, uneasy buoys half sunk in the sea. And they are sunk a bit in the ground. And there is an avenue of mounds, with a sunken path between, parallel to the ravine. This was evidently the grand avenue of the necropolis, like the million-dollar cemetery in New Orleans. *Absit omen!*

Between us and the mounds is a barbed-wire fence. There is a wire gate on which it says you mustn't pick the flowers, whatever that may mean, for there are no flowers. And another notice says, you mustn't tip the guide, as he is gratuitous.

The boys run to the new little concrete house just by, and bring the guide: a youth with red eyes and a bandaged hand. He lost a finger on the railway a month ago. He is shy, and muttering, and neither prepossessing nor cheerful, but he turns out quite decent. He brings keys and an acetylene lamp, and we go through the wire gate into the place of tombs.

There is a queer stillness and a curious peaceful repose about the Etruscan places I have been to, quite different from the weirdness of Celtic places, the slightly repellent feeling of Rome and the old Campagna, and the rather horrible feeling of the great pyramid places in Mexico, Teotihuacan and Cholula, and Mitla in the south; or the amiably idolatrous Buddha places in Ceylon. There is a stillness and a softness in these great grassy mounds with their ancient stone girdles, and down the central walk there lingers still a kind of homeliness and happiness. True, it was a still and

23

sunny afternoon in April, and larks rose from the soft grass of the tombs. But there was a stillness and a soothingness in all the air, in that sunken place, and a feeling that it was good for one's soul to be there.

The same when we went down the few steps, and into the chambers of rock, within the tumulus. There is nothing left. It is like a house that has been swept bare: the inmates have left: now it waits for the next comer. But whoever it is that has departed, they have left a pleasant feeling behind them, warm to the heart, and kindly to the bowels.

They are surprisingly big and handsome, these homes of the dead. Cut out of the living rock, they are just like houses. The roof has a beam cut to imitate the roof-beam of the house. It is a house, a home.

As you enter, there are two small chambers, one to the right, one to the left, antechambers. They say that here the ashes of the slaves were deposited, in urns, upon the great benches of rock. For the slaves were always burned, presumably. Whereas at Cerveteri the masters were laid full-length, sometimes in the great stone sarcophagi, sometimes in big coffins of terra-cotta, in all their regalia. But most often they were just laid there on the broad rock-bed that goes round the tomb, and is empty now, laid there calmly upon an open bier, not shut in sarcophagi, but sleeping as if in life.

The central chamber is large; perhaps there is a

great square column of rock left in the centre, apparently supporting the solid roof as a roof-tree supports the roof of a house. And all round the chamber goes the broad bed of rock, sometimes a double tier, on which the dead were laid, in their coffins, or lying open upon carved litters of stone or wood, a man glittering in golden armour, or a woman in white and crimson robes, with great necklaces round their necks, and rings on their fingers. Here lay the family, the great chiefs and their wives, the Lucumones, and their sons and daughters, many in one tomb.

Beyond again is a rock doorway, rather narrow, and narrowing upwards, like Egypt. The whole thing suggests Egypt; but on the whole, here all is plain, simple, usually with no decoration, and with those easy, natural proportions whose beauty one hardly notices, they come so naturally, physically. It is the natural beauty of proportion of the phallic consciousness, contrasted with the more studied or ecstatic proportion of the mental and spiritual Consciousness we are accustomed to.

Through the inner doorway is the last chamber, small and dark and culminative. Facing the door goes the stone bed on which was laid, presumably, the Lucumo and the sacred treasures of the dead, the little bronze ship of death that should bear him over to the other world, the vases of jewels for his arraying, the vases of small dishes, the little bronze statuettes and tools, the weapons, the armour: all the amazing impedimenta of the important dead. Or sometimes in this inner room lay the woman, the great lady, in all her robes, with the mirror in her hand, and her treasures, her jewels and combs and silver boxes of cosmetics, in urns or vases ranged alongside. Splendid was the array they went with, into death.

One of the most important tombs is the tomb of the Tarquins, the family that gave Etruscan kings to early Rome. You go down a flight of steps, and into the underworld home of the Tarchne, as the Etruscans wrote it. In the middle of the great chamber there are two pillars, left from the rock. The walls of the big living-room of the dead Tarquins, if one may put it so, are stuccoed, but there are no paintings. Only there are the writings on the wall, and in the burial niches in the wall above the long double-tier stone bed ; little sentences freely written in red paint or black, or scratched in the stucco with the finger, slanting with the real Etruscan carelessness and fullness of life, often running downwards, written from right to left. We can read these debonair inscriptions, that look as if someone had just chalked them up yesterday without a thought, in the archaic Etruscan letters, quite easily. But when we have read them we don't know what they mean. *Avle—Tarchnas—Larthal—Clan.* That is plain enough. But what does it mean? Nobody knows precisely. Names, family names, family connections, titles of the dead—we may assume so much. " Aule, son of Larte Tarchna," say the scientists, having got so far. But we cannot read one single sentence. The Etruscan language is a mystery. Yet in Caesar's day it was the everyday language of the bulk of the people in central Italy—at least, east-central. And many Romans spoke Etruscan as we speak French. Yet now the language is entirely lost. Destiny is a queer thing.

The tomb called the Grotta Bella is interesting because of the low-relief carvings and stucco reliefs on the pillars and the walls round the burial niches and above the stone death-bed that goes round the tomb. The things represented are mostly warriors' arms and insignia: shields, helmets, corselets, greaves for the legs, swords, spears, shoes, belts, the necklace of the noble: and then the sacred drinking bowl, the sceptre, the dog who is man's guardian even on the death journey, the two lions that stand by the gateway of life or death, the triton, or merman, and the goose, the bird that swims on the waters and thrusts its head deep into the flood of the Beginning and the End. All these are represented on the walls. And all these, no doubt, were laid, the actual objects, or figures to represent them, in this tomb. But now nothing is left. But when we remember the great store of treasure that every notable tomb must have contained: and that every large tumulus covered several tombs: and that in the necropolis of Cerveteri we can still discover hundreds of tombs: and that other tombs exist in great numbers on the other side of the old city, towards the sea; we can have an idea of the vast mass of wealth this city could afford to bury with its dead, in days when Rome had very little gold, and even bronze was precious.

The tombs seem so easy and friendly, cut out of rock underground. One does not feel oppressed, descending into them. It must be partly owing to the peculiar charm of natural proportion which is in all Etruscan things of the unspoilt, unromanized centuries. There is a simplicity, combined with a most peculiar, free-breasted naturalness and spontaneity, in the shapes and movements of the underworld walls and spaces, that at once reassures the spirit. The Greeks sought to make an impression, and Gothic still more seeks to impress the mind. The Etruscans, no. The things they did, in their easy centuries, are as natural and as easy as breathing. They leave the breast breathing freely and pleasantly, with a certain fullness of life. Even the tombs. And that is the true Etruscan quality : ease, naturalness, and an abundance of life, no need to force the mind or the soul in any direction.

And death, to the Etruscan, was a pleasant continuance of life, with jewels and wine and flutes playing for the dance. It was neither an ecstasy of bliss, a heaven, nor a purgatory of torment. It was just a natural continuance of the fullness of life. Everything was in terms of life, of living.

Yet everything Etruscan, save the tombs, has been wiped out. It seems strange. One goes out again into the April sunshine, into the sunken road between the soft, grassy-mounded tombs, and as one passes one glances down the steps at the doorless doorways of tombs. It is so still and pleasant and cheerful. The place is so soothing.

B., who has just come back from India, is so surprised to see the phallic stones by the doors of many tombs. Why, it's like the Shiva lingam at Benares! It's exactly like the lingam stones in the Shiva caves and the Shiva temples!

And that is another curious thing. One can live one's life, and read all the books about India or Etruria, and never read a single word about the thing that impresses one in the very first five minutes, in Benares or in an Etruscan necropolis: that is, the phallic symbol. Here it is, in stone, unmistakable, and everywhere, around these tombs. Here it is, big and little, standing by the doors, or inserted, quite small, into the rock: the phallic stone! Perhaps some tumuli had a great phallic column on the summit: some perhaps by the door. There are still small phallic stones, only seven or eight inches long, inserted in the rock outside the doors: they always seem to have been outside. And these small lingams look as if they were part of the rock. But no, B. lifts one out. It is cut, and is fitted into a socket, previously cemented in. B. puts the phallic stone back into its socket, where it was placed, probably, five or six hundred years before Christ was born.

The big phallic stones that, it is said, probably stood on top of the tumuli, are sometimes carved very beautifully, sometimes with inscriptions. The scientists call them *cippus*, *cippi*. But surely the cippus is a truncated column used usually as a gravestone: a column quite squat, often square, having been cut across, truncated, to represent maybe a life cut short. Some of the little phallic stones are like this—truncated. But others are tall, huge and decorated, and with the double cone that is surely phallic. And little inserted phallic stones are not cut short.

By the doorway of some tombs there is a carved stone house, or a stone imitation chest with sloping lids like the two sides of the roof of an oblong house. The guide-boy, who works on the railway and is no profound scholar, mutters that every woman's tomb had one of these stone houses or chests over it—over the doorway, he says—and every man's tomb had one of the phallic stones, or lingams. But since the great tombs were family tombs, perhaps they had both.

The stone house, as the boy calls it, suggests the Noah's Ark without the boat part: the Noah's Ark box we had as children, full of animals. And that is what it is, the Ark, the *arx*, the womb. The womb of all the world, that brought forth all the creatures. The womb, the *arx*, where life retreats in the last refuge. The womb, the ark of the covenant, in which lies the mystery of eternal life, the manna and the mysteries.

There it is, standing displaced outside the doorway of Etruscan tombs at Cerveteri.

And perhaps in the insistence on these two symbols, in the Etruscan world, we can see the reason for the utter destruction and annihilation of the Etruscan consciousness. The new world wanted to rid itself of these fatal, dominant symbols of the old world, the old physical world. The Etruscan consciousness was rooted quite blithely in these symbols, the phallus and the arx. So the whole consciousness, the whole Etruscan pulse and rhythm, must be wiped out.

Now we see again, under the blue heavens where the larks are singing in the hot April sky, why the Romans called the Etruscans vicious. Even in their palmy days the Romans were not exactly saints. But they thought they ought to be. They hated the phallus and the ark, because they wanted empire and dominion and, above all, riches: social gain. You cannot dance gaily to the double flute and at the same time conquer nations or rake in large sums of money. *Delenda est Cartago.* To the greedy man, everybody that is in the way of his greed is vice incarnate.

There are many tombs, though not many of the great mounds are left. Most have been levelled. There are many tombs: some were standing half full of water: some were in process of being excavated, in a kind of quarry-place, though the work for the time was silent and abandoned. Many tombs, many, many, and you must descend to them all, for they are all cut

31

out below the surface of the earth; and where there was a tumulus it was piled above them afterwards, loose earth, within the girdle of stone. Some tumuli have been levelled, yet the whole landscape is lumpy with them. But the tombs remain, here all more or less alike, though some are big and some are small, and some are noble and some are rather mean. But most of them seem to have several chambers, beyond the antechambers. And all these tombs along the dead highway would seem to have been topped, once, by the beautiful roundness of tumuli, the great mounds of fruition, for the dead, with the tall phallic cone rising from the summit.

The necropolis, as far as we are concerned, ends on a waste place of deserted excavations and flood-water. We turn back, to leave the home of dead Etruscans. All the tombs are empty. All have been rifled. The Romans may have respected the dead, for a certain time, while their religion was sufficiently Etruscan to exert a power over them. But later, when the Romans started collecting Etruscan antiques—as we collect antiques to-day—there must have been a great sacking of the tombs. Even when all the gold and silver and jewels had been pilfered from the urns—which no doubt happened very soon after the Roman dominion —still the vases and the bronze must have remained in their places. Then the rich Romans began to collect vases, " Greek " vases with the painted scenes. So these were stolen from the tombs. Then the little bronze figures, statuettes, animals, bronze ships, of which the Etruscans put thousands in the tombs, became the rage with the Roman collectors. Some smart Roman gentry would have a thousand or two choice little Etruscan bronzes to boast of. Then Rome fell, and the barbarians pillaged whatever was left. So it went on.

And still some tombs remained virgin, for the earth had washed in and filled the entrance way, covered the stone bases of the mounds; trees, bushes grew over the graves; you had only hilly, humpy, bushy waste country.

Under this the tombs lay silent, either ravaged, or, in a few wonderful cases, still virgin. And still absolutely virgin lay one of the tombs of Cerveteri, alone and apart from the necropolis, buried on the other side of the town, until 1836, when it was discovered: and, of course, denuded. General Galassi and the arch-priest Regolini unearthed it : so it is called the Regolini-Galassi tomb.

It is still interesting: a primitive narrow tomb like a passage, with a partition half-way, and covered with an arched roof, what they call the false arch, which is made by letting the flat horizontal stones of the roof jut out step by step, as they pile upwards, till they almost meet. Then big flat stones are laid as cover, and make the flat top of the almost Gothic arch : an arch built, probably, in the eighth century before Christ.

c

In the first chamber lay the remains of a warrior, with his bronze armour, beautiful and sensitive as if it had grown in life for the living body, sunk on his dust. In the inner chamber beautiful, frail, pale-gold jewellery lay on the stone bed, ear-rings where the ears were dust, bracelets in the dust that once was arms, surely of a noble lady, nearly three thousand years ago.

They took away everything. The treasure, so delicate and sensitive and wistful, is mostly in the Gregorian Museum in the Vatican. On two of the little silver vases from the Regolini-Galassi tomb is the scratched inscription—*Mi Larthia*. Almost the first written Etruscan words we know. And what do they mean, anyhow? "This is Larthia "—Larthia being a lady?

Caere, even seven hundred years before Christ, must have been rich and full of luxury, fond of soft gold and of banquets, dancing, and great Greek vases. But you will find none of it now. The tombs are bare : what treasure they yielded up, and even to us Cerveteri has yielded a great deal, is in the museums. If you go you will see, as I saw, a grey, forlorn little township in tight walls—perhaps having a thousand inhabitants— and some empty burying places.

But when you sit in the post-automobile, to be rattled down to the station, about four o'clock in the sunny afternoon, you will probably see the bus surrounded by a dozen buxom, handsome women, saying good-bye to one of their citizenesses. And in the full, dark, handsome, jovial faces surely you see the lustre still of the life-loving Etruscans! There are some level Greek eyebrows. But surely there are other vivid, warm faces still jovial with Etruscan vitality, beautiful with the mystery of the unrifled ark, ripe with the phallic knowledge and the Etruscan carelessness!

II
TARQUINIA

II

IN Cerveteri there is nowhere to sleep, so the only thing to do is to go back to Rome, or forwards to Cività Vecchia. The bus landed us at the station of Palo at about five o'clock: in the midst of nowhere: to meet the Rome train. But we were going on to Tarquinia, not back to Rome, so we must wait two hours, till seven.

In the distance we could see the concrete villas and new houses of what was evidently Ladispoli, a seaside place, some two miles away. So we set off to walk to Ladispoli, on the flat sea-road. On the left, in the wood that forms part of the great park, the nightingales had already begun to whistle, and looking over the wall one could see many little rose-coloured cyclamens glowing on the earth in the evening light.

We walked on, and the Rome train came surging round the bend. It misses Ladispoli, whose two miles of branch line runs only in the hot bathing months. As we neared the first ugly villas on the road the ancient wagonette drawn by the ancient white horse, both looking sun-bitten almost to ghostliness, clattered past. It just beat us.

Ladispoli is one of those ugly little places on the Roman coast, consisting of new concrete villas, new

39

concrete hotels, kiosks and bathing establishments;
bareness and non-existence for ten months in the year,
seething solid with fleshy bathers in July and August.
Now it was deserted, quite deserted, save for two or
three officials and four wild children.

B. and I lay on the grey-black lava sand, by the
flat, low sea, over which the sky, grey and shapeless,
emitted a flat, wan evening light. Little waves curled
green out of the sea's dark greyness, from the curious
low flatness of the water. It is a peculiarly forlorn
coast, the sea peculiarly flat and sunken, lifeless-looking,
the land as if it had given its last gasp, and was now
for ever inert.

Yet this is the Tyrrhenian sea of the Etruscans,
where their shipping spread sharp sails, and beat the
sea with slave-oars, roving in from Greece and Sicily,
Sicily of the Greek tyrants; from Cumae, the city of the
old Greek colony of Campania, where the province of
Naples now is; and from Elba, where the Etruscans
mined their iron ore. The Etruscans sailed the seas.
They are even said to have come by sea, from Lydia
in Asia Minor, at some date far back in the dim mists
before the eighth century B.C. But that a whole people,
even a whole host, sailed in the tiny ships of those
days, all at once, to people a sparsely peopled central
Italy, seems hard to imagine. Probably ships did come
—even before Ulysses. Probably men landed on the
strange flat coast, and made camps, and then treated
with the natives. Whether the newcomers were Lydians

or Hittites with hair curled in a roll behind, or men
from Mycenae or Crete, who knows. Perhaps men
of all these sorts came, in batches. For in Homeric
days a restlessness seems to have possessed the Mediterranean basin, and ancient races began shaking
ships like seeds over the sea. More people than
Greeks, or Hellenes, or Indo-Germanic groups, were
on the move.

But whatever little ships were run ashore on the
soft, deep, grey-black volcanic sand of this coast, three
thousand years ago, and earlier, their mariners certainly did not find those hills inland empty of people.
If the Lydians or Hittites pulled up their long little
two-eyed ships on to the beach, and made a camp
behind a bank, in shelter from the wet strong wind,
what natives came down curiously to look at them? For
natives there were, of that we may be certain. Even before the fall of Troy, before even Athens was dreamed
of, there were natives here. And they had huts on the
hills, thatched huts in clumsy groups most probably;
with patches of grain, and flocks of goats and probably
cattle. Probably it was like coming on an old Irish
village, or a village in the Scottish Hebrides in Prince
Charlie's day, to come upon a village of these Italian
aborigines, by the Tyrrhenian sea, three thousand years
ago. But by the time Etruscan history starts in Caere,
some eight centuries b.c., there was certainly more
than a village on the hill. There was a native city, of
that we may be sure; and a busy spinning of linen

and beating of gold, long before the Regolini-Galassi tomb was built.

However that may be, somebody came, and somebody was already here: of that we may be certain: and, in the first place, none of them were Greeks or Hellenes. It was the days before Rome rose up: probably when the first comers arrived it was the days even before Homer. The newcomers, whether they were few or many, seem to have come from the east, Asia Minor or Crete or Cyprus. They were, we must feel, of an old, primitive Mediterranean and Asiatic or Aegean stock. The twilight of the beginning of our history was the nightfall of some previous history, which will never be written. Pelasgian is but a shadow-word. But Hittite and Minoan, Lydian, Carian, Etruscan, these words emerge from shadow, and perhaps from one and the same great shadow come the peoples to whom the names belong.

The Etruscan civilization seems a shoot, perhaps the last, from the prehistoric Mediterranean world, and the Etruscans, newcomers and aborigines alike, probably belonged to that ancient world, though they were of different nations and levels of culture. Later, of course, the Greeks exerted a great influence. But that is another matter.

Whatever happened, the newcomers in ancient central Italy found many natives flourishing in posses-sion of the land. These aboriginals, now ridiculously called Villanovans, were neither wiped out nor sup-

pressed. Probably they welcomed the strangers, whose
pulse was not hostile to their own. Probably the more
highly developed religion of the newcomers was not
hostile to the primitive religion of the aborigines : no
doubt the two religions had the same root. Probably
the aborigines formed willingly a sort of religious
aristocracy from the newcomers : the Italians might
almost do the same to-day. And so the Etruscan world
arose. But it took centuries to arise. Etruria was not
a colony, it was a slowly developed country.

There was never an Etruscan nation : only, in
historical times, a great league of tribes or nations
using the Etruscan language and the Etruscan script—
at least officially—and uniting in their religious feeling
and observances. The Etruscan alphabet seems to have
been borrowed from the old Greeks, apparently from
the Chalcidians of Cumae—the Greek colony just north
of where Naples now is. But the Etruscan language is
not akin to any of the Greek dialects, nor, apparently,
to the Italic. But we don't know. It is probably to a
great extent the language of the old aboriginals of
southern Etruria, just as the religion is in all prob-
ability basically aboriginal, belonging to some vast old
religion of the prehistoric world. From the shadow of
the prehistoric world emerge dying religions that have
not yet invented gods or goddesses, but live by the
mystery of the elemental powers in the Universe, the
complex vitalities of what we feebly call Nature. And
the Etruscan religion was certainly one of these. The

gods and goddesses don't seem to have emerged in any sharp definiteness.

But it is not for me to make assertions. Only, that which half emerges from the dim background of time is strangely stirring; and after having read all the learned suggestions, most of them contradicting one another; and then having looked sensitively at the tombs and the Etruscan things that are left, one must accept one's own resultant feeling.

Ships came along this low, inconspicuous sea, coming up from the Near East, we should imagine, even in the days of Solomon—even, maybe, in the days of Abraham. And they kept on coming. As the light of history dawns and brightens, we see them winging along with their white or scarlet sails. Then, as the Greeks came crowding into colonies in Italy, and the Phoenicians began to exploit the western Mediterranean, we begin to hear of the silent Etruscans, and to see them.

Just north of here Caere founded a port called Pyrgi, and we know that the Greek vessels flocked in, with vases and stuffs and colonists coming from Hellas or from Magna Graecia, and that Phoenician ships came rowing sharply, over from Sardinia, up from Carthage, round from Tyre and Sidon; while the Etruscans had their own fleets, built of timber from the mountains, caulked with pitch from northern Volterra, fitted with sails from Tarquinia, filled with wheat from the bountiful plains, or with the famous Etruscan articles of bronze and iron, which they carried away to Corinth or to Athens or to the ports of Asia Minor. We know of the great and finally disastrous sea-battles with the Phœnicians and the tyrant of Syracuse. And we know that the Etruscans, all except those of Caere, became ruthless pirates, almost like the Moors and the Barbary corsairs later on. This was part of their viciousness, a great annoyance to their loving and harmless neighbours, the law-abiding Romans—who believed in the supreme law of conquest.

However, all this is long ago. The very coast has changed since then. The smitten sea has sunk and fallen back, the weary land has emerged when, apparently, it didn't want to, and the flowers of the coast-line are miserable bathing-places such as Ladispoli and seaside Ostia, desecration put upon desolation, to the triumphant trump of the mosquito.

The wind blew flat and almost chill from the darkening sea, the dead waves lifted small bits of pure green out of the leaden greyness, under the leaden sky. We got up from the dark grey but soft sand, and went back along the road to the station, peered at by the few people and officials who were holding the place together till the next bathers came.

At the station there was general desertedness. But our things still lay untouched in a dark corner of the buffet, and the man gave us a decent little meal of cold meats and wine and oranges. It was already night. The train came rushing in, punctually.

It is an hour or more to Cività Vecchia, which is a port of not much importance, except that from here the regular steamer sails to Sardinia. We gave our things to a friendly old porter, and told him to take us to the nearest hotel. It was night, very dark as we emerged from the station.

And a fellow came furtively shouldering up to me.

"You are foreigners, aren't you?"

"Yes."

"What nationality?"

"English."

"You have your permission to reside in Italy—or your passport?"

"My passport I have—what do you want?"

"I want to look at your passport."

"It's in the valise! And why? Why is this?"

"This is a port, and we must examine the papers of foreigners."

"And why? Genoa is a port, and no one dreams of asking for papers."

I was furious. He made no answer. I told the porter to go on to the hotel, and the fellow furtively followed at our side, half-a-pace to the rear, in the mongrel way these spy-louts have.

In the hotel I asked for a room and registered, and then the fellow asked again for my passport. I wanted to know why he demanded it, what he meant by accosting me outside the station as if I was a criminal, what he meant by insulting us with his requests, when

in any other town in Italy one went unquestioned—
and so forth, in considerable rage.

He did not reply, but obstinately looked as though
he would be venomous if he could. He peered at the
passport—though I doubt if he could make head or
tail of it—asked where we were going, peered at B.'s
passport, half excused himself in a whining, disgusting
sort of fashion, and disappeared into the night. A real
lout.

I was furious. Supposing I had not been carrying
my passport—and usually I don't dream of carrying it
—what amount of trouble would that lout have made
me! Probably I should have spent the night in prison,
and been bullied by half-a-dozen low bullies.

Those poor rats at Ladispoli had seen me and B. go
to the sea and sit on the sand for half-an-hour, then go
back to the train. And this was enough to rouse their
suspicions, I imagine, so they telegraphed to Città
Vecchia. Why are officials always fools? Even when
there is no war on? What could they imagine we
were doing?

The hotel manager, propitious, said there was a very
interesting museum in Città Vecchia, and wouldn't we
stay the next day and see it. "Ah!" I replied. "But
all it contains is Roman stuff, and we don't want to
look at that." It was malice on my part, because the
present regime considers itself purely ancient Roman.
The man looked at me scared, and I grinned at him.
"But what do they mean," I said, "behaving like this

to a simple traveller, in a country where foreigners are invited to travel!" "Ah!" said the porter softly and soothingly. "It is the Roman province. You will have no more of it when you leave the Provincia di Roma." And when the Italians give the soft answer to turn away wrath, the wrath somehow turns away.

We walked for an hour in the dull street of Città Vecchia. There seemed so much suspicion, one would have thought there were several wars on. The hotel manager asked if we were staying. We said we were leaving by the eight-o'clock train in the morning, for Tarquinia.

And, sure enough, we left by the eight-o'clock train. Tarquinia is only one station from Città Vecchia—about twenty minutes over the flat Maremma country, with the sea on the left, and the green wheat growing luxuriantly, the asphodel sticking up its spikes.

We soon saw Tarquinia, its towers pricking up like antennae on the side of a low bluff of a hill, some few miles inland from the sea. And this was once the metropolis of Etruria, chief city of the great Etruscan League. But it died like all the other Etruscan cities, and had a more or less mediaeval rebirth, with a new name. Dante knew it, as it was known for centuries, as Corneto—Corgnetum or Cornetium—and forgotten was its Etruscan past. Then there was a feeble sort of wakening to remembrance a hundred years ago, and the town got Tarquinia tacked on to its Corneto: Corneto-Tarquinia. The Fascist regime, however,

glorying in the Italian origins of Italy, has now struck
out the Corneto, so the town is once more, simply,
Tarquinia. As you come up in the motor-bus from
the station you see the great black letters, on a white
ground, painted on the wall by the city gateway :
Tarquinia. So the wheel of revolution turns. There
stands the Etruscan word—Latinized Etruscan—beside
the mediaeval gate, put up by the Fascist power to
name and unname.

But the Fascists, who consider themselves in all
things Roman, Roman of the Caesars, heirs of Empire
and world power, are beside the mark restoring the
rags of dignity to Etruscan places. For of all the Italian
people that ever lived, the Etruscans were surely the
least Roman. Just as, of all the people that ever rose
up in Italy, the Romans of ancient Rome were surely
the most un-Italian, judging from the natives of to-day.

Tarquinia is only about three miles from the sea.
The omnibus soon runs one up, charges through the
widened gateway, swirls round in the empty space
inside the gateway, and is finished. We descend in the
bare place, which seems to expect nothing. On the
left is a beautiful stone palazzo—on the right is a café,
upon the low ramparts above the gate. The man of
the *Dazio*, the town customs, looks to see if anybody
has brought food-stuffs into the town—but it is a mere
glance. I ask him for the hotel. He says : "Do you
mean to sleep?" I say I do. Then he tells a small boy
to carry my bag and take us to Gentile's.

Nowhere is far off, in these small wall-girdled cities. In the warm April morning the stony little town seems half asleep. As a matter of fact, most of the inhabitants are out in the fields, and won't come in through the gates again till evening. The slight sense of desertedness is everywhere—even in the inn, when we have climbed up the stairs to it, for the ground floor does not belong. A little lad in long trousers, who would seem to be only twelve years old but who has the air of a mature man, confronts us with his chest out. We ask for rooms. He eyes us, darts away for the key, and leads us off upstairs another flight, shouting to a young girl, who acts as chambermaid, to follow on. He shows us two small rooms, opening off a big, desert sort of general assembly room common in this kind of inn. "And you won't be lonely," he says briskly, "because you can talk to one another through the wall. *Toh! Lina!*" He lifts his finger and listens. "*Eh!*" comes through the wall, like an echo, with startling nearness and clearness. "*Fai presto!*" says Albertino. "*È pronto!*" comes the voice of Lina. "*Ecco!*" says Albertino to us. "You hear!" We certainly did. The partition wall must have been butter-muslin. And Albertino was delighted, having reassured us we should not feel lonely nor frightened in the night.

He was, in fact, the most manly and fatherly little hotel manager I have ever known, and he ran the whole place. He was in reality fourteen years old, but stunted. From five in the morning till ten at night he was on the go, never ceasing, and with a queer, abrupt, sideways-darting alacrity that must have wasted a great deal of energy. The father and mother were in the background—quite young and pleasant. But they didn't seem to exert themselves. Albertino did it all. How Dickens would have loved him! But Dickens would not have seen the queer wistfulness, and trustfulness, and courage in the boy. He was absolutely unsuspicious of us strangers. People must be rather human and decent in Tarquinia, even the commercial travellers : who, presumably, are chiefly buyers of agricultural produce, and sellers of agricultural implements and so forth.

We sallied out, back to the space by the gate, and drank coffee at one of the tin tables outside. Beyond the wall there were a few new villas—the land dropped green and quick, to the strip of coast plain and the indistinct, faintly gleaming sea, which seemed somehow not like a sea at all.

I was thinking, if this were still an Etruscan city, there would still be this cleared space just inside the gate. But instead of a rather forlorn vacant lot it would be a sacred clearing, with a little temple to keep it alert.

Myself, I like to think of the little wooden temples of the early Greeks and of the Etruscans : small, dainty, fragile, and evanescent as flowers. We have reached the stage when we are weary of huge stone erections, and we begin to realize that it is better to keep life fluid and changing than to try to hold it fast down in heavy monuments. Burdens on the face of the earth are man's ponderous erections.

The Etruscans made small temples, like little houses with pointed roofs, entirely of wood. But then, outside, they had friezes and cornices and crests of terracotta, so that the upper part of the temple would seem almost made of earthenware, terra-cotta plaques fitted neatly, and alive with freely modelled painted figures in relief, gay dancing creatures, rows of ducks, round faces like the sun, and faces grinning and putting out a big tongue, all vivid and fresh and unimposing. The whole thing small and dainty in proportion, and fresh, somehow charming instead of impressive. There seems to have been in the Etruscan instinct a real desire to preserve the natural humour of life. And that is a task surely more worthy, and even much more difficult in the long run, than conquering the world or sacrificing the self or saving the immortal soul.

Why has mankind had such a craving to be imposed upon? Why this lust after imposing creeds, imposing deeds, imposing buildings, imposing language, imposing works of art? The thing becomes an imposition and a weariness at last. Give us things that are alive and flexible, which won't last too long and become an obstruction and a weariness. Even Michelangelo becomes at last a lump and a burden and a bore. It is so hard to see past him.

Across the space from the café is the Palazzo Vitelleschi, a charming building, now a national museum

—so the marble slab says. But the heavy doors are shut. The place opens at ten, a man says. It is nine-thirty. We wander up the steep but not very long street, to the top.

And the top is a fragment of public garden, and a look-out. Two old men are sitting in the sun, under a tree. We walk to the parapet, and suddenly are looking into one of the most delightful landscapes I have ever seen: as it were, into the very virginity of hilly green country. It is all wheat—green and soft and swooping, swooping down and up, and glowing with green newness, and no houses. Down goes the declivity below us, then swerving the curve and up again, to the neighbouring hill that faces in all its greenness and long-running immaculateness. Beyond, the hills ripple away to the mountains, and far in the distance stands a round peak, that seems to have an enchanted city on its summit.

Such a pure, uprising, unsullied country, in the greenness of wheat on an April morning!—and the queer complication of hills! There seems nothing of the modern world here—no houses, no contrivances, only a sort of fair wonder and stillness, an openness which has not been violated.

The hill opposite is like a distinct companion. The near end is quite steep and wild, with evergreen oaks and scrub, and specks of black-and-white cattle on the slopes of common. But the long crest is green again with wheat, running and drooping to the south.

And immediately one feels : that hill has a soul, it has a meaning.

Lying thus opposite to Tarquinia's long hill, a companion across a suave little swing of valley, one feels at once that, if this is the hill where the living Tarquinians had their gay wooden houses, then that is the hill where the dead lie buried and quick, as seeds, in their painted houses underground. The two hills are as inseparable as life and death, even now, on the sunny, green-filled April morning with the breeze blowing in from the sea. And the land beyond seems as mysterious and fresh as if it were still the morning of Time.

But B. wants to go back to the Palazzo Vitelleschi : it will be open now. Down the street we go, and sure enough the big doors are open, several officials are in the shadowy courtyard entrance. They salute us in the Fascist manner : *alla Romana!* Why don't they discover the Etruscan salute, and salute us *all'Etrusca!* But they are perfectly courteous and friendly. We go into the courtyard of the palace.

The museum is exceedingly interesting and delightful, to anyone who is even a bit aware of the Etruscans. It contains a great number of things found at Tarquinia, and important things.

If only we would realize it, and not tear things from their settings. Museums anyhow are wrong. But if one must have museums, let them be small, and above all, let them be local. Splendid as the Etruscan museum is in Florence, how much happier one is in the museum at Tarquinia, where all the things are Tarquinian, and at least have some association with one another, and form some sort of *organic* whole.

In an entrance room from the cortile lie a few of the long sarcophagi in which the nobles were buried. It seems as if the primitive inhabitants of this part of Italy always burned their dead, and then put the ashes in a jar, sometimes covering the jar with the dead man's helmet, sometimes with a shallow dish for a lid, and then laid the urn with its ashes in a little round grave like a little well. This is called the Villanovan way of burial, in the well-tomb.

The newcomers to the country, however, apparently buried their dead whole. Here, at Tarquinia, you may still see the hills where the well-tombs of the aboriginal inhabitants are discovered, with the urns containing the ashes inside. Then come the graves where the dead were buried unburned, graves very much like those of to-day. But tombs of the same period with cinerary urns are found near to, or in connection. So that the new people and the old apparently lived side by side in harmony, from very early days, and the two modes of burial continued side by side, for centuries, long before the painted tombs were made.

At Tarquinia, however, the main practice seems to have been, at least from the seventh century on, that the nobles were buried in the great sarcophagi, or laid out on biers, and placed in chamber-tombs, while the slaves apparently were cremated, their ashes laid in urns, and the urns often placed in the family tomb, where the stone coffins of the masters rested. The common people, on the other hand, were apparently sometimes cremated, sometimes buried in graves very much like our graves of to-day, though the sides were lined with stone. The mass of the common people was mixed in race, and the bulk of them were probably serf-peasants, with many half-free artisans. These must have followed their own desire in the matter of burial : some had graves, many must have been cremated, their ashes saved in an urn or jar which takes up little room in a poor man's burial-place. Probably even the less important members of the noble families were cremated, and their remains placed in the vases, which became more beautiful as the connection with Greece grew more extensive.

It is a relief to think that even the slaves—and the luxurious Etruscans had many, in historical times— had their remains decently stored in jars and laid in a sacred place. Apparently the " vicious Etruscans " had nothing comparable to the vast dead-pits which lay outside Rome, beside the great highway, in which the bodies of slaves were promiscuously flung.

It is all a question of sensitiveness. Brute force and overbearing may make a terrific effect. But in the end, that which lives lives by delicate sensitiveness. If it were a question of brute force, not a single human baby would survive for a fortnight. It is the grass of the field, most frail of all things, that supports all life all the time. But for the green grass, no empire would rise, no man would eat bread: for grain is grass; and Hercules or Napoleon or Henry Ford would alike be denied existence.

Brute force crushes many plants. Yet the plants rise again. The Pyramids will not last a moment compared with the daisy. And before Buddha or Jesus spoke the nightingale sang, and long after the words of Jesus and Buddha are gone into oblivion the nightingale still will sing. Because it is neither preaching nor teaching nor commanding nor urging. It is just singing. And in the beginning was not a Word, but a chirrup.

Because a fool kills a nightingale with a stone, is he therefore greater than the nightingale? Because the Roman took the life out of the Etruscan, was he therefore greater than the Etruscan? Not he! Rome fell, and the Roman phenomenon with it. Italy to-day is far more Etruscan in its pulse than Roman: and will always be so. The Etruscan element is like the grass of the field and the sprouting of corn, in Italy: it will always be so. Why try to revert to the Latin-Roman mechanism and suppression?

In the open room upon the courtyard of the Palazzo Vitelleschi lie a few sarcophagi of stone, with the effigies carved on top, something as the dead crusaders in English churches. And here, in Tarquinia, the effigies are more like crusaders than usual, for some

lie flat on their backs, and have a dog at their feet;
whereas usually the carved figure of the dead rears up
as if alive, from the lid of the tomb, resting upon one
elbow, and gazing out proudly, sternly. If it is a
man, his body is exposed to just below the navel, and
he holds in his hand the sacred *patera*, or *mundum*,
the round saucer with the raised knob in the centre,
which represents the round germ of heaven and earth.
It stands for the plasm, also, of the living cell, with its
nucleus, which is the indivisible God of the beginning,
and which remains alive and unbroken to the end, the
eternal quick of all things, which yet divides and sub-
divides, so that it becomes the sun of the firmament
and the lotus of the waters under the earth, and the
rose of all existence upon the earth: and the sun
maintains its own quick, unbroken for ever; and there
is a living quick of the sea, and of all the waters; and
every living created thing has its own unfailing quick.
So within each man is the quick of him, when he is a
baby, and when he is old, the same quick; some spark,
some unborn and undying vivid life-electron. And
this is what is symbolized in the *patera*, which may be
made to flower like a rose or like the sun, but which
remains the same, the germ central within the living
plasm.

And this *patera*, this symbol, is almost invariably
found in the hand of a dead man. But if the dead is a
woman her dress falls in soft gathers from her throat,
she wears splendid jewellery, and she holds in her

hand not the *mundum*, but the mirror, the box of
essence, the pomegranate, some symbols of her reflected nature, or of her woman's quality. But she, too,
is given a proud, haughty look, as is the man : for
she belongs to the sacred families that rule and that
read the signs.

These sarcophagi and effigies here all belong to the
centuries of the Etruscan decline, after there had been
long intercourse with the Greeks, and perhaps most of
them were made after the conquest of Etruria by the
Romans. So that we do not look for fresh, spontaneous
works of art, any more than we do in modern memorial
stones. The funerary arts are always more or less
commercial. The rich man orders his sarcophagus
while he is still alive, and the monument-carver makes
the work more or less elaborate, according to the price.
The figure is supposed to be a portrait of the man
who orders it, so we see well enough what the later
Etruscans look like. In the third and second centuries
B.C., at the fag end of their existence as a people, they
look very like the Romans of the same day, whose
busts we know so well. And often they are given the
tiresomely haughty air of people who are no longer
rulers indeed, only by virtue of wealth.

Yet, even when the Etruscan art is Romanized and
spoilt, there still flickers in it a certain naturalness
and feeling. The Etruscan *Lucumones*, or prince-
magistrates, were in the first place religious seers,
governors in religion, then magistrates ; then princes.

They were not aristocrats in the Germanic sense, nor even patricians in the Roman. They were first and foremost leaders in the sacred mysteries, then magistrates, then men of family and wealth. So there is always a touch of vital life, of life-significance. And you may look through modern funerary sculpture in vain for anything so good even as the Sarcophagus of the Magistrate, with his written scroll spread before him, his strong, alert old face gazing sternly out, the necklace of office round his neck, the ring of rank on his finger. So he lies, in the museum at Tarquinia. His robe leaves him naked to the hip, and his body lies soft and slack, with the soft effect of relaxed flesh the Etruscan artists render so well, and which is so difficult. On the sculptured side of the sarcophagus the two death-dealers wield the hammer of death, the winged figures wait for the soul, and will not be persuaded away. Beautiful it is, with the easy simplicity of life. But it is late in date. Probably this old Etruscan magistrate is already an official under Roman authority : for he does not hold the sacred *mundum*, the dish, he has only the written scroll, probably of laws. As if he were no longer the religious lord or Lucumo. Though possibly, in this case, the dead man was not one of the Lucumones anyhow.

Upstairs in the museum are many vases, from the ancient crude pottery of the Villanovans to the early black ware decorated in scratches, or undecorated, called *bucchero*, and on to the painted bowls and

dishes and amphoras which came from Corinth or
Athens, or to those painted pots made by the Etruscans
themselves more or less after the Greek patterns. These
may or may not be interesting: the Etruscans are
not at their best, painting dishes. Yet they must have
loved them. In the early days these great jars and
bowls, and smaller mixing bowls, and drinking cups
and pitchers, and flat wine-cups formed a valuable part
of the household treasure. In very early times the
Etruscans must have sailed their ships to Corinth and
to Athens, taking perhaps wheat and honey, wax and
bronze-ware, iron and gold, and coming back with
these precious jars, and stuffs, essences, perfumes and
spice. And jars brought from overseas for the sake
of their painted beauty must have been household
treasures.

But then the Etruscans made pottery of their own,
and by the thousand they imitated the Greek vases.
So that there must have been millions of beautiful jars
in Etruria. Already in the first century B.C. there was
a passion among the Romans for collecting Greek and
Etruscan painted jars from the Etruscans, particularly
from the Etruscan tombs: jars and the little bronze
votive figures and statuettes, the *sigilla Tyrrhena* of the
Roman luxury. And when the tombs were first robbed,
for gold and silver treasure, hundreds of fine jars must
have been thrown over and smashed. Because even
now, when a part-rifled tomb is discovered and opened,
the fragments of smashed vases lie around.

As it is, however, the museums are full of vases. If one looks for the Greek form of elegance and convention, those elegant " still-unravished brides of quietness," one is disappointed. But get over the strange desire we have for elegant convention, and the vases and dishes of the Etruscans, especially many of the black bucchero ware, begin to open out like strange flowers, black flowers with all the softness and the rebellion of life against convention, or red-and-black flowers painted with amusing free, bold designs. It is there nearly always in Etruscan things, the naturalness verging on the commonplace, but usually missing it, and often achieving an originality so free and bold, and so fresh, that we, who love convention and things " reduced to a norm," call it a bastard art, and commonplace.

It is useless to look in Etruscan things for " uplift." If you want uplift, go to the Greek and the Gothic. If you want mass, go to the Roman. But if you love the odd spontaneous forms that are never to be standardized, go to the Etruscans. In the fascinating little Palazzo Vitelleschi one could spend many an hour, but for the fact that the very fullness of museums makes one rush through them.

III

THE PAINTED TOMBS OF
TARQUINIA

III

I

WE arranged for the guide to take us to the painted tombs, which are the real fame of Tarquinia. After lunch we set out, climbing to the top of the town, and passing through the south-west gate, on the level hill-crest. Looking back, the wall of the town, mediaeval, with a bit of more ancient black wall lower down, stands blank. Just outside the gate are one or two forlorn new houses, then ahead, the long, running tableland of the hill, with the white highway dipping and going on to Viterbo, inland.

"All this hill in front," said the guide, "is tombs! All tombs! The city of the dead."

So! Then this hill is the necropolis hill! The Etruscans never buried their dead within the city walls. And the modern cemetery and the first Etruscan tombs lie almost close up to the present city gate. Therefore, if the ancient city of Tarquinia lay on this hill, it can have occupied no more space, hardly, than the present little town of a few thousand people. Which seems impossible. Far more probably, the city itself lay on that opposite hill there, which lies splendid and unsullied, running parallel to us.

We walk across the wild bit of hilltop, where the

stones crop out, and the first rock-rose flutters, and the asphodels stick up. This is the necropolis. Once it had many a tumulus, and streets of tombs. Now there is no sign of any tombs : no tumulus, nothing but the rough bare hill-crest, with stones and short grass and flowers, the sea gleaming away to the right, under the sun, and the soft land inland glowing very green and pure.

But we see a little bit of wall, built perhaps to cover a water-trough. Our guide goes straight towards it. He is a fat, good-natured young man, who doesn't look as if he would be interested in tombs. We are mistaken, however. He knows a good deal, and has a quick, sensitive interest, absolutely unobtrusive, and turns out to be as pleasant a companion for such a visit as one could wish to have.

The bit of wall we see is a little hood of masonry with an iron gate, covering a little flight of steps leading down into the ground. One comes upon it all at once, in the rough nothingness of the hillside. The guide kneels down to light his acetylene lamp, and his old terrier lies down resignedly in the sun, in the breeze which rushes persistently from the south-west, over these long, exposed hilltops.

The lamp begins to shine and smell, then to shine without smelling : the guide opens the iron gate, and we descend the steep steps down into the tomb. It seems a dark little hole underground : a dark little hole, after the sun of the upper world! But the guide's lamp begins to flare up, and we find ourselves in a little chamber in the rock, just a small, bare little cell of a room that some anchorite might have lived in. It is so small and bare and familiar, quite unlike the rather splendid spacious tombs at Cerveteri.

But the lamp flares bright, we get used to the change of light, and see the paintings on the little walls. It is the Tomb of Hunting and Fishing, so called from the pictures on the walls, and it is supposed to date from the sixth century B.C. It is very badly damaged, pieces of the wall have fallen away, damp has eaten into the colours, nothing seems to be left. Yet in the dimness we perceive flights of birds flying through the haze, with the draught of life still in their wings. And as we take heart and look closer we see the little room is frescoed all round with hazy sky and sea, with birds flying and fishes leaping, and little men hunting, fishing, rowing in boats. The lower part of the wall is all a blue-green of sea with a silhouette surface that ripples all round the room. From the sea rises a tall rock, off which a naked man, shadowy but still distinct, is beautifully and cleanly diving into the sea, while a companion climbs up the rock after him, and on the water a boat waits with rested oars in it, three men watching the diver, the middle man standing up naked, holding out his arms. Meanwhile a great dolphin leaps behind the boat, a flight of birds soars upwards to pass the rock, in the clear air. Above all, from the bands of colour that border the wall at the

top hang the regular loops of garlands, garlands of
flowers and leaves and buds and berries, garlands
which belong to maidens and to women, and which
represent the flowery circle of the female life and sex.
The top border of the wall is formed of horizontal
stripes or ribands of colour that go all round the
room, red and black and dull gold and blue and prim-
rose, and these are the colours that occur invariably.
Men are nearly always painted a darkish red, which
is the colour of many Italians when they go naked in
the sun, as the Etruscans went. Women are coloured
paler, because women did not go naked in the sun.

At the end of the room, where there is a recess in
the wall, is painted another rock rising from the sea,
and on it a man with a sling is taking aim at the birds
which rise scattering this way and that. A boat with
a big paddle oar is holding off from the rock, a naked
man amidships is giving a queer salute to the slinger,
a man kneels over the bows with his back to the others,
and is letting down a net. The prow of the boat has
a beautifully painted eye, so the vessel shall see where
it is going. In Syracuse you will see many a two-
eyed boat to-day come swimming in to quay. One
dolphin is diving down into the sea, one is leaping out.
The birds fly, and the garlands hang from the border.

It is all small and gay and quick with life, spontaneous as only young life can be. If only it were not
so much damaged, one would be happy, because here
is the real Etruscan liveliness and naturalness. It is

not impressive or grand. But if you are content with just a sense of the quick ripple of life, then here it is.

The little tomb is empty, save for its shadowy paintings. It has no bed of rock around it: only a deep niche for holding vases, perhaps vases of precious things. The sarcophagus stood on the floor, perhaps under the slinger on the end wall. And it stood alone, for this is an individual tomb, for one person only, as is usual in the older tombs of this necropolis.

In the gable triangle of the end wall, above the slinger and the boat, the space is filled in with one of the frequent Etruscan banqueting scenes of the dead. The dead man, sadly obliterated, reclines upon his banqueting couch with his flat wine-dish in his hand, resting on his elbow, and beside him, also half risen, reclines a handsome and jewelled lady in fine robes, apparently resting her left hand upon the naked breast of the man, and in her right holding up to him the garland—the garland of the female festive offering. Behind the man stands a naked slave-boy, perhaps with music, while another naked slave is just filling a wine-jug from a handsome amphora or wine-jar at the side. On the woman's side stands a maiden, apparently playing the flute: for a woman was supposed to play the flute at classic funerals; and beyond sit two maidens with garlands, one turning round to watch the banqueting pair, the other with her back to it all. Beyond the maidens in the corner are more garlands, and two birds, perhaps doves. On the wall behind the head of the banqueting lady is a problematic object, perhaps a bird-cage.

The scene is natural as life, and yet it has a heavy archaic fullness of meaning. It is the death-banquet; and at the same time it is the dead man banqueting in the underworld; for the underworld of the Etruscans was a gay place. While the living feasted out of doors, at the tomb of the dead, the dead himself feasted in like manner, with a lady to offer him garlands and slaves to bring him wine, away in the underworld. For the life on earth was so good, the life below could but be a continuance of it.

This profound belief in life, acceptance of life, seems characteristic of the Etruscans. It is still vivid in the painted tombs. There is a certain dance and glamour in all the movements, even in those of the naked slave-men. They are by no means downtrodden menials, let later Romans say what they will. The slaves in the tombs are surging with full life.

We come up the steps into the upper world, the sea-breeze and the sun. The old dog shambles to his feet, the guide blows out his lamp and locks the gate, we set off again, the dog trundling apathetic at his master's heels, the master speaking to him with that soft Italian familiarity which seems so very different from the spirit of Rome, the strong-willed Latin.

The guide steers across the hilltop, in the clear afternoon sun, towards another little hood of masonry. And one notices there is quite a number of these little gateways, built by the Government to cover the steps that lead down to the separate small tombs. It is utterly unlike Cerveteri, though the two places are not forty miles apart. Here there is no stately tumulus city, with its highroad between the tombs, and inside, rather noble, many-roomed houses of the dead. Here the little one-room tombs seem scattered at random on the hilltop, here and there: though probably, if excavations were fully carried out, here also we should find a regular city of the dead, with its streets and crossways. And probably each tomb had its little tumulus of piled earth, so that even above-ground there were streets of mounds with tomb entrances. But even so, it would be different from Cerveteri, from Caere; the mounds would be so small, the streets surely irregular. Anyhow, to-day there are scattered little one-room tombs, and we dive down into them just like rabbits popping down a hole. The place is a warren.

It is interesting to find it so different from Cerveteri. The Etruscans carried out perfectly what seems to be the Italian instinct: to have single, independent cities, with a certain surrounding territory, each district speaking its own dialect and feeling at home in its own little capital, yet the whole confederacy of city-states loosely linked together by a common religion and a more-or-less common interest. Even to-day Lucca is very different from Ferrara, and the language is hardly the same. In ancient Etruria this isolation

of cities developing according to their own idiosyn-
crasy, within the loose union of a so-called nation,
must have been complete. The contact between the
plebs, the mass of the people, of Caere and Tarquinii
must have been almost null. They were, no doubt,
foreigners to one another. Only the Lucumones, the
ruling sacred magistrates of noble family, the priests
and the other nobles, and the merchants, must have
kept up an intercommunion, speaking " correct "
Etruscan, while the people, no doubt, spoke dialects
varying so widely as to be different languages. To get
any idea of the pre-Roman past we must break up
the conception of oneness and uniformity, and see an
endless confusion of differences.

We are diving down into another tomb, called, says
the guide, the Tomb of the Leopards. Every tomb
has been given a name, to distinguish it from its neighbours. The Tomb of the Leopards has two spotted
leopards in the triangle of the end wall, between the
roof-slopes. Hence its name.

The Tomb of the Leopards is a charming, cosy little
room, and the paintings on the walls have not been
so very much damaged. All the tombs are ruined to
some degree by weather and vulgar vandalism, having
been left and neglected like common holes, when they
had been broken open again and rifled to the last gasp.

But still the paintings are fresh and alive: the
ochre-reds and blacks and blues and blue-greens are
curiously alive and harmonious on the creamy yellow

walls. Most of the tomb walls have had a thin coat
of stucco, but it is of the same paste as the living rock,
which is fine and yellow, and weathers to a lovely
creamy gold, a beautiful colour for a background.

The walls of this little tomb are a dance of real
delight. The room seems inhabited still by Etruscans
of the sixth century before Christ, a vivid, life-accepting
people, who must have lived with real fullness. On
come the dancers and the music-players, moving in a
broad frieze towards the front wall of the tomb, the
wall facing us as we enter from the dark stairs, and
where the banquet is going on in all its glory. Above
the banquet, in the gable angle, are the two spotted
leopards, heraldically facing each other across a little
tree. And the ceiling of rock has chequered slopes of
red and black and yellow and blue squares, with a
roof-beam painted with coloured circles, dark red and
blue and yellow. So that all is colour, and we do not
seem to be underground at all, but in some gay
chamber of the past.

The dancers on the right wall move with a strange,
powerful alertness onwards. They are men dressed
only in a loose coloured scarf, or in the gay handsome
chlamys draped as a mantle. The *subulo* plays the
double flute the Etruscans loved so much, touching
the stops with big, exaggerated hands, the man behind
him touches the seven-stringed lyre, the man in front
turns round and signals with his left hand, holding
a big wine-bowl in his right. And so they move on,

on their long, sandalled feet, past the little berried olive-trees, swiftly going with their limbs full of life, full of life to the tips.

This sense of vigorous, strong-bodied liveliness is characteristic of the Etruscans, and is somehow beyond art. You cannot think of art, but only of life itself, as if this were the very life of the Etruscans, dancing in their coloured wraps with massive yet exuberant naked limbs, ruddy from the air and the sea-light, dancing and fluting along through the little olive-trees, out in the fresh day.

The end wall has a splendid banqueting scene. The feasters recline upon a checked or tartan couch-cover, on the banqueting couch, and in the open air, for they have little trees behind them. The six feasters are bold and full of life like the dancers, but they are strong, they keep their life so beautifully and richly inside themselves, they are not loose, they don't lose themselves even in their wild moments. They lie in pairs, man and woman, reclining equally on the couch, curiously friendly. The two end women are called *hetaerae*, courtesans; chiefly because they have yellow hair, which seems to have been a favourite feature in a woman of pleasure. The men are dark and ruddy, and naked to the waist. The women, sketched in on the creamy rock, are fair, and wear thin gowns, with rich mantles round their hips. They have a certain free bold look, and perhaps really are courtesans.

The man at the end is holding up, between thumb

74

and forefinger, an egg, showing it to the yellow-
haired woman who reclines next to him, she who is
putting out her left hand as if to touch his breast.
He, in his right hand, holds a large wine-dish, for the
revel.

The next couple, man and fair-haired woman, are
looking round and making the salute with the right
hand curved over, in the usual Etruscan gesture. It
seems as if they too are saluting the mysterious egg
held up by the man at the end; who is, no doubt,
the man who has died, and whose feast is being
celebrated. But in front of the second couple a naked
slave with a chaplet on his head is brandishing an
empty wine-jug, as if to say he is fetching more wine.
Another slave farther down is holding out a curious
thing like a little axe, or fan. The last two feasters are
rather damaged. One of them is holding up a garland
to the other, but not putting it over his head, as they
still put a garland over your head, in India, to honour
you.

Above the banqueters, in the gable angle, the two
great spotted male leopards hang out their tongues and
face each other heraldically, lifting a paw, on either
side of a little tree. They are the leopards or panthers
of the underworld Bacchus, guarding the exits and the
entrances of the passion of life.

There is a mystery and a portentousness in the
simple scenes which go deeper than commonplace
life. It seems all so gay and light. Yet there is a

certain weight, or depth of significance that goes beyond aesthetic beauty.

If one once starts looking, there is much to see. But if one glances merely, there is nothing but a pathetic little room with unimposing, half-obliterated, scratchy little paintings in tempera.

There are many tombs. When we have seen one, up we go, a little bewildered, into the afternoon sun, across a tract of rough, tormented hill, and down again to the underground, like rabbits in a warren. The hilltop is really a warren of tombs. And gradually the underworld of the Etruscans becomes more real than the above day of the afternoon. One begins to live with the painted dancers and feasters and mourners, and to look eagerly for them.

A very lovely dance tomb is the *Tomba del Triclinio*, or *del Convito*, both of which mean: Tomb of the Feast. In size and shape this is much the same as the other tombs we have seen. It is a little chamber about fifteen feet by eleven, six feet high at the walls, about eight feet at the centre. It is again a tomb for one person, like nearly all the old painted tombs here. So there is no inner furnishing. Only the farther half of the rock-floor, the pale yellow-white rock, is raised two or three inches, and on one side of this raised part are the four holes where the feet of the sarcophagus stood. For the rest, the tomb has only its painted walls and ceiling.

And how lovely these have been, and still are! The

band of dancing figures that go round the room still is bright in colour, fresh, the women in thin spotted dresses of linen muslin and coloured mantles with fine borders, the men merely in a scarf. Wildly the bacchic woman throws back her head and curves out her long, strong fingers, wild and yet contained within herself, while the broad-bodied young man turns round to her, lifting his dancing hand to hers till the thumbs all but touch. They are dancing in the open, past little trees, and birds are running, and a little fox-tailed dog is watching something with the naïve intensity of the young. Wildly and delightedly dances the next woman, every bit of her, in her soft boots and her bordered mantle, with jewels on her arms; till one remembers the old dictum, that every part of the body and of the *anima* shall know religion, and be in touch with the gods. Towards her comes the young man piping on the double flute, and dancing as he comes. He is clothed only in a fine linen scarf with a border, that hangs over his arms, and his strong legs dance of themselves, so full of life. Yet, too, there is a certain solemn intensity in his face, as he turns to the woman beyond him, who swoops in a bow to him as she vibrates her castanets.

She is drawn fair-skinned, as all the women are, and he is of a dark red colour. That is the convention, in the tombs. But it is more than convention. In the early days men smeared themselves with scarlet when they took on their sacred natures. The Red Indians still do it. When they wish to figure in their sacred and portentous selves they smear their bodies all over with red. That must be why they are called Red Indians. In the past, for all serious or solemn occasions, they rubbed red pigment into their skins. And the same to-day. And to-day, when they wish to put strength into their vision, and to see true, they smear round their eyes with vermilion, rubbing it into the skin. You may meet them so, in the streets of the American towns.

It is a very old custom. The American Indian will tell you: "The red paint, it is medicine, make you see!" But he means medicine in a different sense from ours. It is deeper even than magic. Vermilion is the colour of his sacred or potent or god body. Apparently it was so in all the ancient world. Man all scarlet was his bodily godly self. We know the kings of ancient Rome, who were probably Etruscans, appeared in public with their faces painted vermilion with minium. And Ezekiel says (xxiii. 14, 15): "She saw men pourtrayed upon the wall, the images of the Chaldeans pourtrayed with vermilion . . . all of them princes to look to, after the manner of the Babylonians of Chaldea, the land of their nativity."

It is then partly a convention, and partly a symbol, with the Etruscans, to represent their men red in colour, a strong red. Here in the tombs everything is in its sacred or inner-significant aspect. But also the red colour is not so very unnatural. When the Italian to-day goes almost naked on the beach he becomes of a lovely dark ruddy colour, dark as any Indian. And the Etruscans went a good deal naked. The sun painted them with the sacred minium.

The dancers dance on, the birds run, at the foot of a little tree a rabbit crouches in a bunch, bunched with life. And on the tree hangs a narrow, fringed scarf, like a priest's stole; another symbol.

The end wall has a banqueting scene, rather damaged, but still interesting. We see two separate couches, and a man and a woman on each. The woman this time is dark-haired, so she need not be a courtesan. The Etruscans shared the banqueting bench with their wives; which is more than the Greeks or Romans did, at this period. The classic world thought it indecent for an honest woman to recline as the men did, even at the family table. If the woman appeared at all, she must sit up straight, in a chair.

Here, the women recline calmly with the men, and one shows a bare foot at the end of the dark couch. In front of the *lecti*, the couches, is in each case a little low square table bearing delicate dishes of food for the feasters. But they are not eating. One woman is lifting her hand to her head in a strange salute to the robed piper at the end, the other woman seems with the lifted hand to be saying No! to the charming maid, perhaps a servant, who stands at her side, presumably offering the *alabastron*, or ointment-jar, while the man at the end apparently is holding up an egg.

Wreaths hang from the ivy-border above, a boy is bringing a wine-jug, the music goes on, and under the beds a cat is on the prowl, while an alert cock watches him. The silly partridge, however, turns his back, stepping innocently along.

This lovely tomb has a pattern of ivy and ivy berries, the ivy of the underworld Bacchus, along the roof-beam and in a border round the top of the walls. The roof-slopes are chequered in red and black, white, blue, brown and yellow squares. In the gable angle, instead of the heraldic beasts, two naked men are sitting reaching back to the centre of an ivy-covered altar, arm outstretched across the ivy. But one man is almost obliterated. At the foot of the other man, in the tight angle of the roof, is a pigeon, the bird of the soul that coos out of the unseen.

This tomb has been open since 1830, and is still fresh. It is interesting to see, in Fritz Weege's book, *Etruskische Malerei*, a reproduction of an old water-colour drawing of the dancers on the right wall. It is a good drawing, yet, as one looks closer, it is quite often out, both in line and position. These Etruscan paintings, not being in our convention, are very difficult to copy. The picture shows my rabbit all spotted, as if it were some queer cat. And it shows a squirrel in the little tree in front of the piper, and flowers, and many details that have now disappeared.

But it is a good drawing, unlike some that Weege reproduces, which are so Flaxmanized and Greekified ;

and made according to what our great-grandfathers thought they *ought* to be, as to be really funny, and a warning for ever against thinking how things *ought* to be, when already they are quite perfectly what they are.

We climb up to the world, and pass for a few minutes through the open day. Then down we go again. In the Tomb of the Bacchanti the colours have almost gone. But still we see, on the end wall, a strange wondering dancer out of the mists of time carrying his zither, and beyond him, beyond the little tree, a man of the dim ancient world, a man with a short beard, strong and mysteriously male, is reaching for a wild archaic maiden who throws up her hands and turns back to him her excited, subtle face. It is wonderful, the strength and mystery of old life that comes out of these faded figures. The Etruscans are still there, upon the wall.

Above the figures, in the gable angle, two spotted deer are prancing heraldically towards one another, on either side the altar, and behind them two dark lions, with pale manes and with tongues hanging out, are putting up a paw to seize them on the haunch. So the old story repeats itself.

From the striped border rude garlands are hanging, and on the roof are little painted stars, or four-petalled flowers. So much has vanished! Yet even in the last breath of colour and form, how much life there is!

In the *Tomba del Morto*, the Tomb of the Dead Man, the banqueting scene is replaced by a scene, apparently, of a dead man on his bed, with a woman leaning gently over to cover his face. It is almost like a banquet scene. But it is so badly damaged! In the gable above, two dark heraldic lions are lifting the paw against two leaping, frightened, backward-looking birds. This is a new variation. On the broken wall are the dancing legs of a man, and there is more life in these Etruscan legs, fragment as they are, than in the whole bodies of men to-day. Then there is one really impressive dark figure of a naked man who throws up his arms so that his great wine-bowl stands vertical, and with spread hand and closed face gives a strange gesture of finality. He has a chaplet on his head, and a small pointed beard, and lives there shadowy and significant.

Lovely again is the *Tomba delle Leonesse*, the Tomb of the Lionesses. In its gable two spotted lionesses swing their bell-like udders, heraldically facing one another across the altar. Beneath is a great vase, and a flute-player playing to it on one side, a zither-player on the other, making music to its sacred contents. Then on either side of these goes a narrow frieze of dancers, very strong and lively in their prancing. Under the frieze of dancers is a lotus dado, and below that again, all round the room, the dolphins are leaping, leaping all downwards into the rippling sea, while birds fly between the fishes.

On the right wall reclines a very impressive dark red man wearing a curious cap, or head-dress, that has long tails like long plaits. In his right hand he holds

up an egg, and in his left is the shallow wine-bowl of
the feast. The scarf or stole of his human office hangs
from a tree before him, and the garland of his human
delight hangs at his side. He holds up the egg of
resurrection, within which the germ sleeps as the soul
sleeps in the tomb, before it breaks the shell and
emerges again. There is another reclining man, much
obliterated, and beside him hangs a garland or chain
like the chains of dandelion-stems we used to make as
children. And this man has a naked flute-boy, lovely
in naked outline, coming towards him.

The *Tomba della Pulcella*, or Tomb of the Maiden,
has faded but vigorous figures at the banquet, and very
ornate couch-covers in squares and the key-pattern, and
very handsome mantles.

The *Tomba dei Vasi Dipinti*, Tomb of the Painted
Vases, has great amphorae painted on the side wall,
and springing towards them is a weird dancer, the
ends of his waist-cloth flying. The amphorae, two of
them, have scenes painted on them, which can still be
made out. On the end wall is a gentle little banquet
scene, the bearded man softly touching the woman
with him under the chin, a slave-boy standing childishly
behind, and an alert dog under the couch. The *kylix*,
or wine-bowl, that the man holds is surely the biggest
on record; exaggerated, no doubt, to show the very
special importance of the feast. Rather gentle and
lovely is the way he touches the woman under the
chin, with a delicate caress. That again is one of the

charms of the Etruscan paintings: they really have the sense of touch; the people and the creatures are all really in touch. It is one of the rarest qualities, in life as well as in art. There is plenty of pawing and laying hold, but no real touch. In pictures especially, the people may be in contact, embracing or laying hands on one another. But there is no soft flow of touch. The touch does not come from the middle of the human being. It is merely a contact of surfaces, and a juxtaposition of objects. This is what makes so many of the great masters boring, in spite of all their clever composition. Here, in this faded Etruscan painting, there is a quiet flow of touch that unites the man and the woman on the couch, the timid boy behind, the dog that lifts his nose, even the very garlands that hang from the wall.

Above the banquet, in the triangle, instead of lions or leopards we have the hippocampus, a favourite animal of the Etruscan imagination. It is a horse that ends in a long, flowing fish-tail. Here these two hippocampi face one another prancing their front legs, while their fish-tails flow away into the narrow angle of the roof. They are a favourite symbol of the seaboard Etruscans.

In the *Tomba del Vecchio*, the Tomb of the Old Man, a beautiful woman with her hair dressed backwards into the long cone of the East, so that her head is like a sloping acorn, offers her elegant, twisted garland to the white-bearded old man, who is now beyond garlands. He lifts his left hand up at her, with the rich gesture of these people, that must mean something each time.

Above them, the prancing spotted deer are being seized in the haunch by two lions. And the waves of obliteration, wastage of time and damage of men, are silently passing over all.

So we go on, seeing tomb after tomb, dimness after dimness, divided between the pleasure of finding so much and the disappointment that so little remains. One tomb after another, and nearly everything faded or eaten away, or corroded with alkali, or broken wilfully. Fragments of people at banquets, limbs that dance without dancers, birds that fly in nowhere, lions whose devouring heads are devoured away! Once it was all bright and dancing; the delight of the under-world; honouring the dead with wine, and flutes playing for a dance, and limbs whirling and pressing. And it was deep and sincere honour rendered to the dead and to the mysteries. It is contrary to our ideas; but the ancients had their own philosophy for it. As the pagan old writer says: "For no part of us nor of our bodies shall be, which doth not feel religion: and let there be no lack of singing for the soul, no lack of leaping and of dancing for the knees and heart; for all these know the gods."

Which is very evident in the Etruscan dancers. They know the gods in their very finger-tips. The wonderful fragments of limbs and bodies that dance on in a field of obliteration still know the gods, and make it evident to us.

But we can hardly see any more tombs. The upper air seems pallid and bodiless, as we emerge once more, white with the light of the sea and the coming evening. And spent and slow the old dog rises once more to follow after.

We decide that the *Tomba delle Iscrizioni*, the Tomb of the Inscriptions, shall be our last for to-day. It is dim but fascinating, as the lamp flares up, and we see in front of us the end wall, painted with a false door studded with pale studs, as if it led to another chamber beyond; and riding from the left, a trail of shadowy tall horsemen; and running in from the right, a train of wild shadowy dancers wild as demons.

The horsemen are naked on the four naked horses, and they make gestures as they come towards the painted door. The horses are alternately red and black, the red having blue manes and hoofs, the black, red ones, or white. They are tall archaic horses on slim legs, with necks arched like a curved knife. And they come pinking daintily and superbly along, with their long tails, towards the dark red death-door.

From the left, the stream of dancers leaps wildly, playing music, carrying garlands or wine-jugs, lifting their arms like revellers, lifting their live knees, and signalling with their long hands. Some have little inscriptions written near them: their names.

And above the false door in the angle of the gable

is a fine design: two black, wide-mouthed, pale-maned lions seated back to back, their tails rising like curved stems, between them, as they each one lift a black paw against the cringing head of a cowering spotted deer, that winces to the death-blow. Behind each deer is a smaller dark lion, in the acute angle of the roof, coming up to bite the shrinking deer in the haunch, and so give the second death-wound. For the wounds of death are in the neck and in the flank.

At the other end of the tomb are wrestlers and gamesters; but so shadowy now! We cannot see any more, nor look any further in the shadows for the unconquerable life of the Etruscans, whom the Romans called vicious, but whose life, in these tombs, is certainly fresh and cleanly vivid.

The upper air is wide and pale, and somehow void. We cannot see either world any more, the Etruscan underworld nor the common day. Silently, tired, we walk back in the wind to the town, the old dog padding stoically behind. And the guide promises to take us to the other tombs to-morrow.

There is a haunting quality in the Etruscan representations. Those leopards with their long tongues hanging out: those flowing hippocampi; those cringing spotted deer, struck in flank and neck; they get into the imagination, and will not go out. And we see the wavy edge of the sea, the dolphins curving over, the diver going down clean, the little man climbing up the rock after him so eagerly. Then the men with beards who recline on the banqueting beds : how they hold up the mysterious egg! And the women with the conical head-dress, how strangely they lean forward, with caresses we no longer know! The naked slaves joyfully stoop to the wine-jars. Their nakedness is its own clothing, more easy than drapery. The curves of their limbs show pure pleasure in life, a pleasure that goes deeper still in the limbs of the dancers, in the big, long hands thrown out and dancing to the very ends of the fingers, a dance that surges from within, like a current in the sea. It is as if the current of some strong different life swept through them, different from our shallow current to-day: as if they drew their vitality from different depths that we are denied.

Yet in a few centuries they lost their vitality. The Romans took the life out of them. It seems as if the power of resistance to life, self-assertion and overbearing, such as the Romans knew: a power which must needs be moral, or carry morality with it, as a cloak for its inner ugliness: would always succeed in destroying the natural flowering of life. And yet there still are a few wild flowers and creatures.

The natural flowering of life! It is not so easy for human beings as it sounds. Behind all the Etruscan liveliness was a religion of life, which the chief men were seriously responsible for. Behind all the dancing was a vision, and even a science of life, a conception

TARQUINIA.   CORNER OF THE CITY WITH CHURCH OF S. MARIA IN CASTELLO

CERVETERI. ENTERANCE TO THE CHAMBER TOMBS

CERVETERI. TERRA-COTTA HEADS ON SARCOPHAGUS
NOW IN THE VILLA GIULLA MUSEUM, ROME

TARQUINIA. GREEK VASES WITH EYE–PATTERN AND HEAD OF BACCHUS

TARQUINIA. TOMB OF LEOPARDS

TARQUINIA. TOMB OF THE FEAST

TARQUINIA. TOMB OF THE BULLS

VOLTERRA. ASH–CHEST SHOWING ACTEON AND THE DOGS

of the universe and man's place in the universe which made men live to the depth of their capacity.

To the Etruscan all was alive; the whole universe lived; and the business of man was himself to live amid it all. He had to draw life into himself, out of the wandering huge vitalities of the world. The cosmos was alive, like a vast creature. The whole thing breathed and stirred. Evaporation went up like breath from the nostrils of a whale, steaming up. The sky received it in its blue bosom, breathed it in and pondered on it and transmuted it, before breathing it out again. Inside the earth were fires like the heat in the hot red liver of a beast. Out of the fissures of the earth came breaths of other breathing, vapours direct from the living physical underearth, exhalations carrying inspiration. The whole thing was alive, and had a great soul, or *anima*: and in spite of one great soul, there were myriad roving, lesser souls; every man, every creature and tree and lake and mountain and stream, was animate, had its own peculiar consciousness. And has it to-day.

The cosmos was one, and its *anima* was one; but it was made up of creatures. And the greatest creature was earth, with its soul of inner fire. The sun was only a reflection, or off-throw, or brilliant handful, of the great inner fire. But in juxtaposition to earth lay the sea, the waters that moved and pondered and held a deep soul of their own. Earth and waters lay side by side, together, and utterly different.

89

So it was. The universe, which was a single aliveness with a single soul, instantly changed, the moment
you thought of it, and became a dual creature with
two souls, fiery and watery, for ever mingling and
rushing apart, and held by the great aliveness of the
universe in an ultimate equilibrium. But they rushed
together and they rushed apart, and immediately they
became myriad; volcanoes and seas, then streams and
mountains, trees, creatures, men. And everything was
dual, or contained its own duality, for ever mingling
and rushing apart.

The old idea of the vitality of the universe was
evolved long before history begins, and elaborated
into a vast religion before we get a glimpse of it.
When history does begin, in China or India, Egypt,
Babylonia, even in the Pacific and in aboriginal America,
we see evidence of one underlying religious idea: the
conception of the vitality of the cosmos, the myriad
vitalities in wild confusion, which still is held in some
sort of array: and man, amid all the glowing welter,
adventuring, struggling, striving for one thing, life,
vitality, more vitality: to get into himself more and
more of the gleaming vitality of the cosmos. That is
the treasure. The active religious idea was that man,
by vivid attention and subtlety and exerting all his
strength, could draw more life into himself, more life,
more and more glistening vitality, till he became
shining like the morning, blazing like a god. When
he was all himself he painted himself vermilion like

the throat of dawn, and was god's body, visibly, red and utterly vivid. So he was a prince, a king, a god, an Etruscan Lucumo; Pharaoh, or Belshazzar, or Ashurbanipal, or Tarquin; in a feebler *decrescendo*, Alexander, or Caesar, or Napoleon.

This was the idea at the back of all the great old civilizations. It was even, half-transmuted, at the back of David's mind, and voiced in the Psalms. But with David the living cosmos became merely a personal god. With the Egyptians and Babylonians and Etruscans, strictly there were no personal gods. There were only idols or symbols. It was the living cosmos itself, dazzlingly and gaspingly complex, which was divine, and which could be contemplated only by the strongest soul, and only at moments. And only the peerless soul could draw into itself some last flame from the quick. Then you had a king-god indeed.

There you have the ancient idea of kings, kings who are gods by vividness, because they have gathered into themselves core after core of vital potency from the universe, till they are clothed in scarlet, they are bodily a piece of the deepest fire. Pharaohs and kings of Nineveh, kings of the East, and Etruscan Lucumones, they are the living clue to the pure fire, to the cosmic vitality. They are the vivid key to life, the vermilion clue to the mystery and the delight of death and life. They, in their own body, unlock the vast treasure-house of the cosmos for their people, and bring out life, and show the way into the dark of death, which is the blue burning of the one fire. They, in their own bodies, are the life-bringers and the death-guides, leading ahead in the dark, and coming out in the day with more than sunlight in their bodies. Can one wonder that such dead are wrapped in gold; or were?

The life-bringers, and the death-guides. But they set guards at the gates both of life and death. They keep the secrets, and safeguard the way. Only a few are initiated into the mystery of the bath of life, and the bath of death: the pool within pool within pool, wherein, when a man is dipped, he becomes darker than blood, with death, and brighter than fire, with life; till at last he is scarlet royal as a piece of living life, pure vermilion.

The people are not initiated into the cosmic ideas, nor into the awakened throb of more vivid consciousness. Try as you may, you can never make the mass of men throb with full awakenedness. They *cannot* be more than a little aware. So you must give them symbols, ritual and gesture, which will fill their bodies with life up to their own full measure. Any more is fatal. And so the actual knowledge must be guarded from them, lest knowing the formulae, without undergoing at all the experience that corresponds, they may become insolent and impious, thinking they have the all, when they have only an empty monkey-chatter. The esoteric knowledge will always be esoteric, since knowledge is an experience, not a formula. But it is foolish to hand out the formulae. A little knowledge

is indeed a dangerous thing. No age proves it more
than ours. Monkey-chatter is at last the most
disastrous of all things.

The clue to the Etruscan life was the Lucumo, the
religious prince. Beyond him were the priests and
warriors. Then came the people and the slaves. People
and warriors and slaves did not think about religion.
There would soon have been no religion left. They
felt the symbols and danced the sacred dances. For
they were always kept *in touch*, physically, with the
mysteries. The "touch" went from the Lucumo
down to the merest slave. The blood-stream was unbroken. But "knowing" belonged to the high-born,
the pure-bred.

So, in the tombs we find only the simple, uninitiated
vision of the people. There is none of the priest-work
of Egypt. The symbols are to the artist just wonder-
forms, pregnant with emotion and good for decoration.
It is so all the way through Etruscan art. The artists
evidently were of the people, artisans. Presumably
they were of the old Italic stock, and understood
nothing of the religion in its intricate form, as it had
come in from the East: though doubtless the crude
principles of the official religion were the same as those
of the primitive religion of the aborigines. The same
crude principles ran through the religions of all the
barbaric world of that time, Druid or Teutonic or
Celtic. But the newcomers in Etruria held secret the
science and philosophy of their religion, and gave the

people the symbols and the ritual, leaving the artists free to use the symbols as they would; which shows that there was no priest-rule.

Later, when scepticism came over all the civilized world, as it did after Socrates, the Etruscan religion began to die, Greeks and Greek rationalism flooded in, and Greek stories more or less took the place of the old Etruscan symbolic thought. Then again the Etruscan artists, uneducated, used the Greek stories as they had used the Etruscan symbols, quite freely, making them over again just to please themselves.

But one radical thing the Etruscan people never forgot, because it was in their blood as well as in the blood of their masters: and that was the mystery of the journey out of life, and into death; the death-journey, and the sojourn in the after-life. The wonder of their soul continued to play round the mystery of this journey and this sojourn.

In the tombs we see it; throes of wonder and vivid feeling throbbing over death. Man moves naked and glowing through the universe. Then comes death: he dives into the sea, he departs into the underworld.

The sea is that vast primordial creature that has a soul also, whose inwardness is womb of all things, out of which all things emerged, and into which they are devoured back. Balancing the sea is the earth of inner fire, of after-life and before-life. Beyond the waters and the ultimate fire lay only that oneness of which the people knew nothing: it was a secret the Lucumones

kept for themselves, as they kept the symbol of it in
their hand.

But the sea the people knew. The dolphin leaps in
and out of it suddenly, as a creature that suddenly
exists, out of nowhere. He was not : and lo ! there he
is ! The dolphin which gives up the sea's rainbows
only when he dies. Out he leaps ; then, with a head-
dive, back again he plunges into the sea. He is so much
alive, he is like the phallus carrying the fiery spark of
procreation down into the wet darkness of the womb.
The diver does the same, carrying like a phallus his
small hot spark into the deeps of death. And the
sea will give up her dead like dolphins that leap out
and have the rainbow within them.

But the duck that swims on the water, and lifts his
wings, is another matter : the blue duck, or goose, so
often represented by the Etruscans. He is the same
goose that saved Rome, in the night.

The duck does not live down within the waters as
the fish does. The fish is the *anima*, the animate life,
the very clue to the vast sea, the watery element of the
first submission. For this reason Jesus was represented
in the first Christian centuries as a fish, in Italy especially, where the people still thought in the Etruscan
symbols. Jesus was the *anima* of the vast, moist ever-
yielding element which was the opposite and the
counterpart of the red flame the Pharaohs and the kings
of the East had sought to invest themselves with.

But the duck has no such subaqueous nature as the

95

fish. It swims upon the waters, and is hot-blooded, belonging to the red flame of the animal body of life. But it dives under water, and preens itself upon the flood. So it became, to man, the symbol of that part of himself which delights in the waters, and dives in, and rises up and shakes its wings. It is the symbol of a man's own phallus and phallic life. So you see a man holding on his hand the hot, soft, alert duck, offering it to the maiden. So to-day the Red Indian makes a secret gift to the maiden of a hollow, earthenware duck, in which is a little fire and incense. It is that part of his body and his fiery life that a man can offer to a maid. And it is that awareness or alertness in him, that other consciousness, that wakes in the night and rouses the city.

But the maid offers the man a garland, the rim of flowers from the edge of the " pool," which can be placed over the man's head and laid on his shoulders, in symbol that he is invested with the power of the maiden's mystery and different strength, the female power. For whatever is laid over the shoulders is a sign of power added.

Birds fly portentously on the walls of the tombs. The artist must often have seen those priests, the augurs, with their crooked, bird-headed staffs in their hand, out on a high place watching the flight of larks or pigeons across the quarters of the sky. They were reading the signs and the portents, looking for an indication, how they should direct the course of some serious affair. To us it may seem foolish. To them, hot-blooded birds flew through the living universe as feelings and premonitions fly through the breast of a man, or as thoughts fly through the mind. In their flight the suddenly roused birds, or the steady, far-coming birds, moved wrapped in a deeper conscious-ness, in the complex destiny of all things. And since all things corresponded in the ancient world, and man's bosom mirrored itself in the bosom of the sky, or *vice versa*, the birds were flying to a portentous goal, in the man's breast who watched, as well as flying their own way in the bosom of the sky. If the augur could see the birds flying *in his heart*, then he would know which way destiny too was flying for him.

The science of augury certainly was no exact science. But it was as exact as our sciences of psychology or political economy. And the augurs were as clever as our politicians, who also must practise divination, if ever they are to do anything worth the name. There is no other way when you are dealing with life. And if you live by the cosmos, you look in the cosmos for your clue. If you live by a personal god, you pray to him. If you are rational, you think things over. But it all amounts to the same thing in the end. Prayer, or thought, or studying the stars, or watching the flight of birds, or studying the entrails of the sacrifice, it is all the same process, ultimately: of divination. All it depends on is the amount of *true*, sincere, religious concentration you can bring to bear on your object. An act of pure attention, if you are capable of it, will bring its own answer. And you choose that object to concentrate upon which will best focus your consciousness. Every real discovery made, every serious and significant decision ever reached, was reached and made by divination. Columbus discovered America by a sort of divination. The soul stirs, and makes an act of pure attention, and that is a discovery.

The science of the augur and the haruspex was not so foolish as our modern science of political economy. If the hot liver of the victim cleared the soul of the haruspex, and made him capable of that ultimate inward attention which alone tells us the last thing we need to know, then why quarrel with the haruspex? To him, the universe was alive, and in quivering *rapport*. To him, the blood was conscious; he thought with his heart. To him, the blood was the red and shining stream of consciousness itself. Hence, to him, the liver, that great organ where the blood struggles and " overcomes death," was an object of profound mystery and significance. It stirred his soul and purified his consciousness; for it was also his victim. So he gazed into the hot liver, that was mapped out in fields and regions like the sky of stars, but these fields and regions were those of the red, shining consciousness that runs through the whole animal creation. And therefore it must contain the answer to his own blood's question.

It is the same with the study of stars, or the sky of

stars. Whatever object will bring the consciousness
into a state of pure attention, in a time of perplexity,
will also give back an answer to the perplexity. But it
is truly a question of *divination*. As soon as there is
any pretence of infallibility, and pure scientific calcula-
tion, the whole thing becomes a fraud and a jugglery.
But the same is true not only of augury and astrology,
but also of prayer and of pure reason, and even of the
discoveries of the great laws and principles of science.
Men juggle with prayer to-day as once they juggled
with augury; and in the same way they are juggling
with science. Every great discovery or decision comes
by an act of divination. Facts are fitted round afterwards. But all attempt at divination, even prayer and
reason and research itself, lapses into jugglery when
the heart loses its purity. In the impurity of his heart,
Socrates often juggled logic unpleasantly. And no
doubt, when scepticism came over the ancient world,
the haruspex and the augur became jugglers and pre-
tenders. But for centuries they held real sway. It is
amazing to see, in Livy, what a big share they must
have had in the building up of the great Rome of the
Republic.

Turning from birds to animals, we find in the tombs
the continual repetition of lion against deer. As soon
as the world was created, according to the ancient idea,
it took on duality. All things became dual, not only
in the duality of sex, but in the polarity of action.
This is the " impious pagan duality." It did not,

99

however, contain the later pious duality of good and evil.

The leopard and the deer, the lion and the bull, the cat and the dove, or the partridge, these are part of the great duality, or polarity of the animal kingdom. But they do not represent good action and evil action. On the contrary, they represent the polarized activity of the divine cosmos, in its animal creation.

The treasure of treasures is the soul, which, in every creature, in every tree or pool, means that mysterious conscious point of balance or equilibrium between the two halves of the duality, the fiery and the watery. This mysterious point clothes itself in vividness after vividness from the right hand, and vividness after vividness from the left. And in death it does not disappear, but is stored in the egg, or in the jar, or even in the tree which brings forth again.

But the soul itself, the conscious spark of every creature, is not dual; and being the immortal, it is also the altar on which our mortality and our duality is at last sacrificed.

So as the key-picture in the tombs, we have over and over again the heraldic beasts facing one another across the altar, or the tree, or the vase; and the lion is smiting the deer in the hip and the throat. The deer is spotted, for day and night, the lion is dark and light the same.

The deer or lamb or goat or cow is the gentle creature with udder of overflowing milk and fertility;

or it is the stag or ram or bull, the great father of the herd, with horns of power set obvious on the brow, and indicating the dangerous aspect of the beasts of fertility. These are the creatures of prolific, boundless procreation, the beasts of peace and increase. So even Jesus is the lamb. And the endless, endless gendering of these creatures will fill all the earth with cattle till herds rub flanks over all the world, and hardly a tree can rise between.

But this must not be so, since they are only half, even of the animal creation. Balance must be kept. And this is the altar we are all sacrificed upon: it is even death; just as it is our soul and purest treasure.

So, on the other hand from the deer, we have lionesses and leopards. These, too, are male and female. These, too, have udders of milk and nourish young; as the wolf nourished the first Romans: prophetically, as the destroyers of many deer, including the Etruscan. So these fierce ones guard the treasure and the gateway, which the prolific ones would squander or close up with too much gendering. They bite the deer in neck and haunch, where the great blood-streams run.

So the symbolism goes all through the Etruscan tombs. It is very much the symbolism of all the ancient world. But here it is not exact and scientific, as in Egypt. It is simple and rudimentary, and the artist plays with it as a child with fairy stories. Nevertheless, it is the symbolic element which rouses the deeper emotion, and gives the peculiarly satisfying quality to the dancing figures and the creatures. A painter like Sargent, for example, is so clever. But in the end he is utterly uninteresting, a bore. He never has an inkling of his own triviality and silliness. One Etruscan leopard, even one little quail, is worth all the miles of him.

IV
THE PAINTED TOMBS OF TARQUINIA

IV

2

WE sit at the tin tables of the café above the gate watching the peasants coming in the evening from the fields, with their implements and their asses. As they drift in through the gate the man of the *Dazio*, the town customs, watches them, asks them questions if they carry bundles, prods the pack on the ass, and when a load of brushwood rolls up keeps it halted while he pierces the load with a long steel rod, carefully thrusting to see if he can feel hidden barrels of wine or demijohns of oil, bales of oranges or any other food-stuffs. Because all food-stuffs that come into an Italian town — many other things too, besides comestibles — must pay a duty, in some instances a heavy one.

Probably in Etruscan days the peasants came in very much the same, at evening, to the town. The Etruscans were instinctively citizens. Even the peasants dwelt within walls. And in those days, no doubt, the peasants were serfs very much as they are to-day in Italy, work-ing the land for no wages, but for a portion of the produce; and working the land intensely, with that careful, almost passionate attention the Italian still gives to the soil; and living in the city, or village, but having straw huts out in the fields, for summer.

But in those days, on a fine evening like this, the men would come in naked, darkly ruddy-coloured from the sun and wind, with strong, insouciant bodies; and the women would drift in, wearing the loose, becoming smock of white or blue linen; and somebody, surely, would be playing on the pipes; and somebody, surely, would be singing, because the Etruscans had a passion for music, and an inner carelessness the modern Italians have lost. The peasants would enter the clear, clean, sacred space inside the gates, and salute the gay-coloured little temple as they passed along the street that rose uphill towards the arx, between rows of low houses with gay-coloured fronts painted or hung with bright terra-cottas. One can almost hear them still, calling, shouting, piping, singing, driving in the mixed flocks of sheep and goats, that go so silently, and leading the slow, white, ghostlike oxen with the yokes still on their necks.

And surely, in those days, young nobles would come splashing in on horseback, riding with naked limbs on an almost naked horse, carrying probably a spear, and cantering ostentatiously through the throng of red-brown, full-limbed, smooth-skinned peasants. A Lucumo, even, sitting very noble in his chariot driven by an erect charioteer, might be driving in at sundown, halting before the temple to perform the brief ritual of entry into the city. And the crowding populace would wait; for the Lucumo of the old days, glowing ruddy in flesh, his beard stiffly trimmed in the Oriental style, the torque of gold round his neck, and the mantle or wrap bordered with scarlet falling in full folds, leaving the breast bare, he was divine, sitting on the chair in his chariot in the stillness of power. The people drew strength even from looking at him.

The chariot drew a little forward, from the temple; the Lucumo, sitting erect on his chair in the chariot, and bare-shouldered and bare-breasted, waits for the people. Then the peasants would shrink back in fear. But perhaps some citizen in a white tunic would lift up his arms in salute, and come forward to state his difficulty, or to plead for justice. And the Lucumo, seated silent within another world of power, disciplined to his own responsibility of knowledge for the people, would listen till the end. Then a few words—and the chariot of gilt bronze swirls off up the hill to the house of the chief, the citizens drift on to their houses, the music sounds in the dark streets, torches flicker, the whole place is eating, feasting, and as far as possible having a gay time.

It is different now. The drab peasants, muffled in ugly clothing, straggle in across the waste bit of space, and trail home, songless and meaningless. We have lost the art of living; and in the most important science of all, the science of daily life, the science of behaviour, we are complete ignoramuses. We have psychology instead. To-day in Italy, in the hot Italian summer, if a navvy working in the street takes off his shirt to work with free, naked torso, a policeman rushes to him and commands him insultingly into his shirt again. One would think a human being was such a foul indecency altogether that life was feasible only when the indecent thing was as far as possible blotted out. The very exposure of female arms and legs in the street is only done as an insult to the whole human body. "Look at that! It doesn't matter!"

Neither does it! But then, why did the torso of the workman matter?

At the hotel, in the dark emptiness of the place, there are three Japanese staying: little yellow men. They have come to inspect the salt works down on the coast below Tarquinia, so we are told, and they have a Government permit. The salt works, the extracting of salt from the pools shut off from the low sea, are sort of prisons, worked by convict labour. One wonders why Japanese men should want to inspect such places, officially. But we are told that these salt works are "very important."

Albertino is having a very good time with the three Japanese, and seems to be very deep in their confidence, bending over their table, his young brown head among the three black ones, absorbed and on the *qui vive*. He rushes off for their food—then rushes to us to see what we want to eat.

"What is there?"

"*Er—c'è*——" He always begins with wonderful deliberation, as if there was a menu fit for the Tsar. Then

he breaks off suddenly, says : " I'll ask the mamma ! "
—darts away—returns, and says exactly what we knew
he'd say, in a bright voice, as if announcing the New
Jerusalem : " There are eggs—er—and beefsteak—er
and there are some little potatoes." We know the
eggs and beefsteak well ! However, I decide to have
beefsteak once more, with the little potatoes—left over
by good fortune from lunch—fried. Off darts Albertino,
only to dart back and announce that the potatoes and
beefsteak are finished (" by the Chinese," he whispers),
" but there are frogs." "There are what ? " " *Le rane*,
the frogs ! " "What sort of frogs ? " " I'll show you ! "
Off he darts again, returns with a plate containing eight
or nine pairs of frogs' naked hind-legs. B. looks the
other way and I accept frogs—they look quite good. In
the joy of getting the frogs safely to port, Albertino
skips, and darts off : to return in a moment with a bottle
of beer, and whisper to us all the information about the
Chinese, as he calls them. They can't speak a word of
Italian. When they want a word they take the little
book, French and Italian. *Bread ?*—eh ? They want
bread. Er !—Albertino gives little grunts, like commas
and semicolons, which I write as *er* ! Bread they want,
eh ?—er !—they take the little book—here he takes an
imaginary little book, lays it on the tablecloth, wets his
finger and turns over the imaginary leaves—*bread !*—
er !—p—you look under ' p '—er !—*ecco ! pane !—pane !*
—*si capisce !*—bread ! they want bread. Then wine !
er ! take the little book (he turns over imaginary

little leaves with fervour)—er! here you are, *vino !—pane, e vino !* So they do! Every word! They looked out name! Er! you! Er! I tell him, *Albertino*. And so the boy continues, till I ask what about *le rane* ? Ah! *Er! Le rane !* Off he darts, and swirls back with a plate of fried frogs' legs, in pairs.

He is an amusing and vivacious boy, yet underneath a bit sad and wistful, with all his responsibility. The following day he darted to show us a book of views of Venice, left behind by the Chinese, as he persists in calling them, and asks if I want it. I don't. Then he shows us two Japanese postage stamps, and the address of one of the Japanese gentlemen, written on a bit of paper. The Japanese gentleman and Albertino are to exchange picture postcards. I insist that the Japanese are not Chinese. "Er!" says Albertino. "But the Japanese are also Chinese!" I insist that they are not, that they live in a different country. He darts off, and returns with a school atlas. "Er! China is in Asia! Asia! Asia!"—he turns the leaves. He is really an intelligent boy, and ought to be going to school instead of running an hotel at the tender age of fourteen.

The guide to the tombs, having had to keep watch at the museum all night, wants to get a sleep after dawn, so we are not to start till ten. The town is already empty, the people gone out to the fields. A few men stand about with nothing doing. The city gates are wide open. At night they are closed, so that the *Dazio* man can sleep: and you can neither get in nor out of

the town. We drink still another coffee—Albertino's
morning dose was a very poor show.

Then we see the guide, talking to a pale young
fellow in old corduroy velveteen knee-breeches and an
old hat and thick boots : most obviously German. We
go over, make proper salutes, nod to the German boy,
who looks as if he'd had vinegar for breakfast—and
set off. This morning we are going out a couple of
miles, to the farthest end of the necropolis. We have
still a dozen tombs to look at. In all, there are either
twenty-five or twenty-seven painted tombs one can
visit.

This morning there is a stiff breeze from the south-
west. But it is blowing fresh and clear, not behaving
in the ugly way the *libeccio* can behave. We march
briskly along the highway, the old dog trundling behind.
He loves spending a morning among the tombs.
The sea gives off a certain clearness, that makes the
atmosphere doubly brilliant and exhilarating, as if we
were on a mountain-top. The omnibus rolls by, from
Viterbo. In the fields the peasants are working, and
the guide occasionally greets the women, who give
him a sally back again. The young German tramps
firmly on : but his spirit is not as firm as his tread.
One doesn't know what to say to him, he vouchsafes
nothing, seems as if he didn't want to be spoken to,
and yet is probably offended that we don't talk to him.
The guide chatters to him in unfailing cheerfulness,
in Italian : but after a while drops back with evident

relief to the milder company of B., leaving me to the young German, who has certainly swallowed vinegar some time or other.

But I feel with him as with most of the young people of to-day: he has been sinned against more than he sins. The vinegar was given him to drink. Breaking reluctantly into German, since Italian seems foolish, and he won't come out in English, I find, within the first half-mile, that he is twenty-three (he looks nineteen), has finished his university course, is going to be an archaeologist, is travelling doing archaeology, has been in Sicily and Tunis, whence he has just returned; didn't think much of either place—*mehr Schrei wie Wert*, he jerks out, speaking as if he were throwing his words away like a cigarette-end he was sick of; doesn't think much of any place; doesn't think much of the Etruscans — *nicht viel Wert*; doesn't, apparently, think much of me; knows a professor or two whom I have met; knows the tombs of Tarquinia very well, having been here, and stayed here, twice before; doesn't think much of them; is going to Greece; doesn't expect to think much of it; is staying in the other hotel, not Gentile's, because it is still cheaper: is probably staying a fortnight, going to photograph all the tombs, with a big photographic apparatus — has the Government authority, like the Japs—apparently has very little money indeed, marvellously doing everything on nothing—expects to be a famous professor in a science he doesn't think

much of—and I wonder if he always has enough
to eat.

He certainly is a fretful and peevish, even if in some
ways silent and stoical, young man. *Nicht viel Wert!*—
not much worth—doesn't amount to anything—seems
to be his favourite phrase, as it is the favourite phrase of
almost all young people to-day. Nothing amounts to
anything, for the young.

Well, I feel it's not my fault, and try to bear up. But
though it is bad enough to have been of the war generation, it must be worse to have grown up just after the
war. One can't blame the young, that they don't find
that anything amounts to anything. The war cancelled
most meanings for them.

And my young man is not really so bad: he would
even rather like to be *made* to believe in something.
There is a yearning pathos in him somewhere.

We have passed the modern cemetery, with its
white marble headstones, and the arches of a mediaeval
aqueduct mysteriously spanning a dip, and left the
highroad, following a path along the long hill-crest,
through the green wheat that flutters and ripples in the
sea-wind like fine feathers, in the wonderful brilliance
of morning. Here and there are tassels of mauve
anemones, bits of verbena, many daisies, tufts of
camomile. On a rocky mound, which was once a
tumulus, the asphodels have the advantage, and send
up their spikes on the bright, fresh air, like soldiers
clustered on the mount. And we go along this vivid

H

green headland of wheat—which still is rough and uneven, because it was once all tumuli—with our faces to the breeze, the sea-brightness filling the air with exhilaration, and all the country still and silent, and we talk German in the wary way of two dogs sniffing at one another.

Till suddenly we turn off to an almost hidden tomb—the German boy knows the way perfectly. The guide hurries up and lights the acetylene lamp, the dog slowly finds himself a place out of the wind, and flings himself down: and we sink slowly again into the Etruscan world, out of the present world, as we descend underground.

One of the most famous tombs at this far-off end of the necropolis is the Tomb of the Bulls. It contains what the guide calls: *un po' di pornografico !*—but a very little. The German boy shrugs his shoulders as usual: but he informs us that this is one of the oldest tombs of all, and I believe him, for it looks so to me.

It is a little wider than some tombs, the roof has not much pitch, there is a stone bed for sarcophagi along the side walls, and in the end wall are two doorways, cut out of the rock of the end and opening into a second chamber, which seems darker and more dismal. The German boy says this second chamber was cut out later, from the first one. It has no paintings of any importance.

We return to the first chamber, the old one. It is called the Tomb of the Bulls from the two bulls above

the doorways of the end wall, one a man-faced bull
charging at the "*po' di pornografico*," the other lying
down serenely and looking with mysterious eyes into
the room, his back turned calmly to the second bit of
a picture which the guide says is not "*pornografico*"—
"because it is a woman." The young German smiles
with his sour-water expression.

Everything in this tomb suggests the old East:
Cyprus, or the Hittites, or the culture of Minos of
Crete. Between the doorways of the end wall is a
charming painting of a naked horseman with a spear,
on a naked horse, moving towards a charming little
palm-tree and a well-head or fountain-head, on which
repose two sculptured, black-faced beasts, lions with
queer black faces. From the mouth of the one near
the palm-tree water pours down into a sort of altar-
bowl, while on the far side a warrior advances,
wearing a bronze helmet and shin-greaves, and apparently menacing the horseman with a sword which
he brandishes in his left hand, as he steps up on to the
base of the well-head. Both warrior and horseman
wear the long, pointed boots of the East: and the
palm-tree is not very Italian.

This picture has a curious charm, and is evidently
symbolical. I said to the German : " What do you think
it means?" "Ach, nothing! The man on the horse
has come to the drinking-trough to water his horse : no
more!" "And the man with the sword?" "Oh, he
is perhaps his enemy." "And the black-faced lions?"

"Ach, nothing! Decorations of the fountain." Below the picture are trees on which hang a garland and a neck-band. The border pattern, instead of the egg and dart, has the sign of Venus, so called, between the darts: a ball surmounted by a little cross. "And that, is that a symbol?" I asked the German. "Here no!" he replied abruptly. "Merely a decoration!"—which is perhaps true. But that the Etruscan artist had no more feeling for it, as a symbol, than a modern house-decorator would have, that we cannot believe.

I gave up for the moment. Above the picture is a sentence lightly written, almost scribbled, in Etruscan. "Can you read it?" I said to the German boy. He read it off quickly—myself, I should have had to go letter by letter. "Do you know what it means?" I asked him. He shrugged his shoulders. "Nobody knows."

In the shallow angle of the roof the heraldic beasts are curious. The squat centre-piece, the so-called altar, has four rams' heads at the corners. On the right a pale-bodied man with a dark face is galloping up with loose rein, on a black horse, followed by a galloping bull. On the left is a bigger figure, a queer galloping lion with his tongue out. But from the lion's shoulders, instead of wings, rises the second neck of a dark-faced, bearded goat: so that the complex animal has a second, backward-leaning neck and head, of a goat, as well as the first maned neck and menacing head of a lion. The tail of the lion ends in a serpent's head. So this is the proper Chimaera. And galloping after the end of the lion's tail comes a winged female sphinx.

"What is the meaning of this lion with the second head and neck?" I asked the German. He shrugged his shoulders, and said: "Nothing!" It meant nothing to him, because nothing except the ABC of facts means anything to him. He is a scientist, and when he doesn't want a thing to have a meaning it is, *ipso facto*, meaningless.

But the lion with the goat's head springing backwards from its shoulders must mean something, because there it is, very vivid, in the famous bronze Chimaera of Arezzo, which is in the Florence museum, and which Benvenuto Cellini restored, and which is one of the most fascinating bronzes in the world. There, the bearded goat's head springs twisting backwards from the lion's shoulders, while the right horn of the goat is seized in the mouth of the serpent, which is the tail of the lion whipped forward over his back.

Though this is the correct Chimaera, with the wounds of Bellerophon in hip and neck, still it is not merely a big toy. It has, and was intended to have, an exact esoteric meaning. In fact, Greek myths are only gross representations of certain very clear and very ancient esoteric conceptions, that are much older than the myths: or the Greeks. Myths, and personal gods, are only the decadence of a previous cosmic religion.

The strange potency and beauty of these Etruscan

things arise, it seems to me, from the profundity of the symbolic meaning the artist was more or less aware of. The Etruscan religion, surely, was never anthropomorphic : that is, whatever gods it contained were not *beings*, but symbols of elemental powers, just symbols : as was the case earlier in Egypt. The undivided Godhead, if we can call it such, was symbolized by the *mundum*, the plasm-cell with its nucleus : that which is the very beginning ; instead of, as with us, by a personal god, a person being the very end of all creation or evolution. So it is all the way through : the Etruscan religion is concerned with all those physical and creative powers and forces which go to the building up and the destroying of the soul : the soul, the personality, being that which gradually is produced out of chaos, like a flower, only to disappear again into chaos, or the underworld. We, on the contrary, say : In the beginning was the Word !—and deny the physical universe true existence. We exist only in the Word, which is beaten out thin to cover, gild, and hide all things.

The human being, to the Etruscan, was a bull or a ram, a lion or a deer, according to his different aspects and potencies. The human being had in his veins the blood of the wings of birds and the venom of serpents. All things emerged from the blood-stream, and the blood-relation, however complex and contradictory it might become, was never interrupted or forgotten. There were different currents in the blood-stream, and some always clashed: bird and serpent, lion and deer, leopard and lamb. Yet the very clash was a form of unison, as we see in the lion which also has a goat's head.

But the young German will have nothing of this. He is a modern, and the obvious alone has true existence for him. A lion with a goat's head as well as its own head is unthinkable. That which is unthinkable is non-existent, is nothing. So, all the Etruscan symbols are to him non-existent and mere crude incapacity to think. He wastes not a thought on them; they are spawn of mental impotence, hence negligible.

But perhaps also he doesn't want to give himself away, or divulge any secret that is going to make him a famous archaeologist later on. Though I don't think that was it. He was very nice, showing me details, with his flashlight, that I should have overlooked. The white horse, for example, has had its drawing most plainly altered: you can see the old outline of the horse's back legs and breast, and of the foot of the rider, and you can see how considerably the artist changed the drawing, sometimes more than once. He seems to have drawn the whole thing complete, each time, then changed the position, changed the direction, to please his feeling. And as there was no indiarubber to rub out the first attempts, there they are, from at least six hundred years before Christ: the delicate mistakes of an Etruscan who had the instinct of a pure artist in him, as well as the blithe insouciance which makes him leave his alterations for anyone to spy out, if they want to.

The Etruscan artists either drew with the brush or scratched, perhaps, with a nail, the whole outline of their figures on the soft stucco, and then applied their colour *al fresco*. So they had to work quickly. Some of the paintings seemed to me tempera, and in one tomb, I think the Francesco Giustiniani, the painting seemed to be done on the naked, creamy rock. In that case, the blue colour of the man's scarf is marvellously vivid.

The subtlety of Etruscan painting, as of Chinese and Hindu, lies in the wonderfully suggestive *edge* of the figures. It is not outlined. It is not what we call " drawing." It is the flowing contour where the body suddenly leaves off, upon the atmosphere. The Etruscan artist seems to have seen living things surging from their own centre to their own surface. And the curving and contour of the silhouette-edge suggests the whole movement of the modelling within. There is actually no modelling. The figures are painted in the flat. Yet they seem of a full, almost turgid muscularity. It is only when we come to the late Tomb of Typhon that we have the figure *modelled*, Pompeian style, with light and shade.

It must have been a wonderful world, that old world where everything appeared alive and shining in the dusk of contact with all things, not merely as an isolated individual thing played upon by daylight; where each thing had a clear outline, visually, but in its very clarity was related emotionally or vitally to strange other things, one thing springing from another, things mentally contradictory fusing together emotionally, so that a lion could be at the same moment also a goat, and not a goat. In those days, a man riding on a red horse was not just Jack Smith on his brown nag; it was a suave-skinned creature, with death or life in its face, surging along on a surge of animal power that burned with travel, with the passionate movement of the blood, and which was swirling along on a mysterious course, to some unknown goal, swirling with a weight of its own. Then also, a bull was not merely a stud animal worth so much, due to go to the butcher in a little while. It was a vast wonder-beast, a well-head of the great, furnace-like passion that makes the worlds roll and the sun surge up, and makes a man surge with procreative force; the bull, the herd-lord, the father of calves and heifers, of cows; the father of milk; he who has the horns of power on his forehead, symbolizing the warlike aspect of the horn of fertility; the bellowing master of force, jealous, horned, charging against opposition. The goat was in the same line, father of milk, but instead of huge force he had cunning, the cunning *consciousness* and self-consciousness of the jealous, hard-headed father of procreation. Whereas the lion was most terrible, yellow and roaring with a blood-drinking energy, again like the sun, but the sun asserting himself in drinking up the life of the earth. For the sun can warm the worlds, like a yellow hen

sitting on her eggs. Or the sun can lick up the life of
the world with a hot tongue. The goat says: let me
breed for ever, till the world is one reeking goat. But
then the lion roars from the other blood-stream, which
is also in man, and he lifts his paw to strike, in the
passion of the other wisdom.

So all creatures are potential in their own way, a
myriad manifold consciousness storming with contradictions and oppositions that are eternal, beyond all
mental reconciliation. We can know the living world
only symbolically. Yet every consciousness, the rage of
the lion, and the venom of the snake, *is*, and therefore
is divine. All emerges out of the unbroken circle with
its nucleus, the germ, the One, the god, if you like to
call it so. And man, with his soul and his personality,
emerges in eternal connection with all the rest. The
blood-stream is one, and unbroken, yet storming with
oppositions and contradictions.

The ancients saw, consciously, as children now see
unconsciously, the everlasting *wonder* in things. In the
ancient world the three compelling emotions must
have been emotions of wonder, fear and admiration:
admiration in the Latin sense of the word, as well as
our sense; and fear in its largest meaning, including
repulsion, dread and hate: then arose the last, individual emotion of pride. Love is only a subsidiary
factor in wonder and admiration.

But it was by seeing all things alert in the throb
of interrelated passional significance that the ancients

kept the wonder and the delight in life, as well as the
dread and the repugnance. They were like children :
but they had the force, the power and the sensual
knowledge of true adults. They had a world of valuable
knowledge, which is utterly lost to us. Where they
were true adults, we are children ; and vice versa.

Even the two bits of ' *pornografico* ' in the Tomb of
the Bull are not two little dirty drawings. Far from it.
The German boy felt this, as we did. The drawings
have the same naïve wonder in them as the rest, the
same archaic innocence, accepting life, knowing all
about it, and *feeling* the meaning, which is like a stone
fallen into consciousness, sending its rings ebbing out
and out, to the extremes. The two little pictures have
a symbolic meaning, quite distinct from a *moral* meaning—or an immoral. The words moral and immoral
have no force. Some acts—what Dennis would call
flagrant obscenity—the man-faced bull accepts calmly
lying down ; against other acts he charges with lowered
horns. It is not judgment. It is the sway of passional
action and reaction : the action and reaction of the
father of milk.

There are beautiful tombs, in this far-off wheat-
covered hill. The Tomb of the Augurs is very impressive. On the end wall is painted a doorway to
a tomb, and on either side of it is a man making
what is probably the mourning gesture, strange and
momentous, one hand to the brow. The two men are
mourning at the door of the tomb.

"No!" says the German. "The painted door does not represent the door to the tomb, with mourners on either side. It is merely the painted door which later they intended to cut out, to make a second chamber to the tomb. And the men are not mourning."

"Then what are they doing?"

Shrug!

In the triangle above the painted door two lions, a white-faced one and a dark-faced, have seized a goat or an antelope: the dark-faced lion turns over and bites the side of the goat's neck, the white-faced bites the haunch. Here we have again the two heraldic beasts: but instead of their roaring at the altar, or the tree, they are biting the goat, the father of milk-giving life, in throat and hip.

On the side walls are very fine frescoes of nude wrestlers, and then of a scene which has started a lot of talk about Etruscan cruelty. A man with his head in a sack, wearing only a skin-girdle, is being bitten in the thigh by a fierce dog which is held, by another man, on a string attached to what is apparently a wooden leash, this wooden handle being fastened to the dog's collar. The man who holds the string wears a peculiar high conical hat, and he stands, big-limbed and excited, striding behind the man with his head in the sack. This victim is by now getting entangled in the string, the long, long cord which holds the dog; but with his left hand he seems to be getting hold of the cord to drag the dog off from his thigh, while in his right hand he holds a huge club, with which to strike the dog when he can get it into striking range.

This picture is supposed to reveal the barbarously cruel sports of the Etruscans. But since the tomb contains an augur, with his curved sceptre, tensely lifting his hand to the dark bird that flies by: and the wrestlers are wrestling over a curious pile of three great bowls; and on the other side of the tomb the man in the conical pointed hat, he who holds the string in the first picture, is now dancing with a peculiar delight, as if rejoicing in victory or liberation: we must surely consider this picture as symbolic, along with all the rest: the fight of the blindfolded man with some raging, attacking element. If it were sport there would be onlookers, as there are at the sports in the Tomb of the Chariots; and here there are none.

However, the scenes portrayed in the tomb are all *so* real, that it seems they must have taken place in actual life. Perhaps there was some form of test or trial which gave a man a great club, tied his head in a sack, and left him to fight a fierce dog which attacked him, but which was held on a string, and which even had a wooden grip-handle attached to its collar, by which the man might seize it and hold it firm, while he knocked it on the head. The man in the sack has very good chances against the dog. And even granted the thing was done for sport, and not as some sort of trial or test, the cruelty is not excessive, for the man has a very good chance of knocking the dog on the head quite early. Compared with Roman gladiatorial shows, this is almost " fair play."

But it must be more than sport. The dancing of the man who held the string is too splendid. And the tomb is, somehow, too intense, too meaningful. And the dog —or wolf or lion—that bites the thigh of the man is too old a symbol. We have it very plainly on the top of the Sarcophagus of the Painted Amazons, in the Florence museum. This sarcophagus comes from Tarquinia—and the end of the lid has a carved naked man, with legs apart, a dog on each side biting him in the thigh. They are the dogs of disease and death, biting at the great arteries of the thigh, where the elementary life surges in a man. The motive is common in ancient symbolism. And the esoteric idea of malevolent influences attacking the great arteries of the thighs was turned in Greece into the myth of Actaeon and his dogs.

Another very fine tomb is the Tomb of the Baron, with its frieze of single figures, dark on a light background, going round the walls. There are horses and men, all in dark silhouette, and very fascinating in drawing. These archaic horses are so perfectly satisfying *as* horses : so far more horselike, to the soul, than those of Rosa Bonheur or Rubens or even Velazquez, though he comes nearer to these ; so that one asks oneself, what, after all, is the horsiness of a horse?

What is it that man sees, when he looks at a horse?
—what is it, that will never be put into words? For a
man who sees, sees not as a camera does when it takes
a snapshot, not even as a cinema-camera, taking its
succession of instantaneous snaps; but in a curious
rolling flood of vision, in which the image itself
seethes and rolls; and only the mind *picks out*
certain factors which *shall* represent the image seen.
That is why a camera is so unsatisfactory: its eye
is flat, it is related only to a negative thing inside
the box: whereas inside our living box there is a
decided positive.

We go from tomb to tomb, down into the dark, up
again into the wind and brilliance; and the day rolls
by. But we are moving, tomb by tomb, gradually
nearer the city. The new cemetery draws near. We
have passed the aqueduct, which crosses the dip, then
takes an underground channel towards the town. Near
the cemetery we descend into a big tomb, the biggest
we have yet seen—a great underground cavern with
great wide beds for sarcophagi and biers, and in the
centre a massive square pillar or shaft on which is
painted a Typhon—the seaman with coiled snake-legs,
and wings behind his arms, his hands holding up the
roof; two Typhons, another on the opposite face of
the pillar, almost identical with the first.

In this place, almost at once, the Etruscan charm
seems to vanish. The tomb is big, crude, somehow
ugly, like a cavern. The Typhon, with his reddish

flesh and light-and-shade modelling, is clever, and might be modern, done for effect. He is rather Pompeian—and a little like Blake. But he is done from quite a new consciousness, external; the old inwardness has gone. Dennis, who saw him eighty years ago, thinks him far more marvellous than the archaic dancers. But we do not.

There are some curly-wig dolphins sporting over a curly border which, but for experience, we should not know was the sea. And there is a border of "roses," really the sacred symbol of the "one" with its central germ, here for the first time vulgarly used. There is also a fragment of a procession to Hades, which must have been rather fine in the Graeco-Roman style. But the true archaic charm is utterly gone. The dancing Etruscan spirit is dead.

This is one of the very latest tombs: said to be of the second century B.C., when the Romans had long been masters of Tarquinia. Veii, the first great Etruscan city to be captured by Rome, was taken about 388 B.C., and completely destroyed. From then on, Etruria gradually weakened and sank, till the peace of 280 B.C., when we may say the military conquest of Etruria was complete.

So that the tombs suddenly change. Those supposed to be of the fifth century, like the Tomb of the Baron, with the frieze of horses and men, or the Tomb of the Leopards, are still perfectly Etruscan, no matter what touch of the Orient they may have, and perfectly charming. Then suddenly we come to the Tomb of Orcus, or Hell, which is given the fourth century as a date, and here the whole thing utterly changes. You get a great gloomy, clumsy, rambling sort of under-world, damp and horrid, with large but much-damaged pictures on the walls.

These paintings, though they are interesting in their way, and have scribbled Etruscan inscriptions, have suddenly lost all Etruscan charm. They still have a bit of Etruscan freedom, but on the whole they are Graeco-Roman, half suggesting Pompeian, half suggesting Roman things. They are more free than the paintings of the little old tombs; at the same time, all the motion is gone; the figures are stuck there without any vital flow between them. There is no touch.

Instead of the wonderful old silhouette forms we have modern " drawing," often quite good. But to me it is an intense disappointment.

When the Roman took the power from the hands of the Etruscan Lucumones—in the fourth century B.C. —and made them merely Roman magistrates, at the best, the mystery of Etruria died almost at once. In the ancient world of king-gods, governing accord-ing to a religious conception, the deposition of the chiefs and the leading priests leaves the country at once voiceless and mindless. So it was in Egypt and Babylonia, in Assyria, in the Aztec and Maya lordships of America. The people are governed by the flower of the race. Pluck the flower, and the race is helpless.

The Etruscans were not destroyed. But they lost their being. They had lived, ultimately, by the *subjective* control of the great natural powers. Their subjective power fell before the objective power of the Romans. And almost at once the true race-consciousness finished. The Etruscan knowledge became mere superstition. The Etruscan princes became fat and inert Romans. The Etruscan people became expressionless and meaningless. It happened amazingly quickly, in the third and second centuries B.C.

Yet the Etruscan *blood* continued to beat. And Giotto and the early sculptors seem to have been a flowering again of the Etruscan blood, which is always putting forth a flower, and always being trodden down again by some superior " force." It is a struggle between the endless patience of life and the endless triumph of force.

There is one other huge late tomb, the Tomb of the Shields, said to be of the third century. It contains many fragmentary paintings. There is a banqueting scene, with a man on the banqueting bench taking the egg from the woman, and she is touching his shoulder. But they might as well be two chairs from a " suite." There is nothing between them. And they have those " important " sort of faces—all on the outside, nothing inside—that are so boring. Yet they are interesting. They might almost be done to-day, by an

ultra-modern artist bent on being absolutely childlike
and naïve and archaic. But after the real archaic paintings, these are empty. The air is empty. The egg is
still held up. But it means no more to that man and
woman than the chocolate Easter egg does to us. It
has gone cold.

In the Tomb of Orcus begins that representation
of the grisly underworld, hell and its horrors, which
surely was reflected on to the Etruscans from the grisly
Romans. The lovely little tombs of just one small
chamber, or perhaps two chambers, of the earlier
centuries give way to these great sinister caverns
underground, and hell is fitly introduced.

The old religion of the profound attempt of man to
harmonize himself with nature, and hold his own and
come to flower in the great seething of life, changed
with the Greeks and Romans into a desire to resist
nature, to produce a mental cunning and a mechanical
force that would outwit Nature and chain her down
completely, completely, till at last there should be
nothing free in nature at all, all should be controlled,
domesticated, put to man's meaner uses. Curiously
enough, with the idea of the triumph over nature arose
the idea of a gloomy Hades, a hell and purgatory.
To the peoples of the great natural religions the
after-life was a continuing of the wonder-journey of
life. To the peoples of the Idea the after-life is hell,
or purgatory, or nothingness, and paradise is an
inadequate fiction.

But, naturally enough, historians seized on these essentially non-Etruscan evidences, in the Etruscan late tombs, to build up a picture of a gloomy, hellish, serpent-writhing, vicious Etruscan people who were quite rightly stamped out by the noble Romans. This myth is still not dead. Men *never* want to believe the evidence of their senses. They would far rather go on elaborating some " classical " author. The whole science of history seems to be the picking of old fables and old lies into fine threads, and weaving them up again. Theopompus collected some scandalous tales, and that is quite enough for historians. It is written down, so that's enough. The evidence of fifty million gay little tombs wouldn't weigh a straw. In the beginning was the Word, indeed! Even the word of a Theopompus!

Perhaps the favourite painting for representing the beauties of the Etruscan tombs is the well-known head of a woman, seen in profile with wheat-ears for a head-wreath, or fillet. This head comes from the Tomb of Orcus, and is chosen because it is far more Greek-Roman than it is Etruscan. As a matter of fact, it is rather stupid and self-conscious—and modern. But it belongs to the classic Convention, and men can only see according to a Convention. We haven't exactly plucked our eyes out, but we've plucked out three-fourths of their vision.

After the Tomb of the Typhon one has had enough. There is nothing really Etruscan left. It is better to

abandon the necropolis altogether, and to remember
that almost everything we know of the Etruscans from
the classic authors is comparable to the paintings in the
late tombs. It refers only to the fallen, Romanized
Etruscans of the decadence.

It is very pleasant to go down from the hill on which
the present Tarquinia stands, down into the valley and
up to the opposite hill, on which the Etruscan Tarquinii
surely stood. There are many flowers, the blue grape-
hyacinth and the white, the mauve tassel anemone,
and, in a corner of a field of wheat, the big purple
anemone, then a patch of the big pale pink anemone
with the red, sore centre—the big-petalled sort. It is
curious how the anemone varies. Only in this one
place in Tarquinia have I found the whity-pink kind,
with the dark, sore-red centre. But probably that is
just chance.

The town ends really with the wall. At the foot of
the wall is wild hillside, and down the slope is only one
little farm, with another little house made of straw. The
country is clear of houses. The peasants live in the city.

Probably in Etruscan days it was much the same, but
there must have been far more people on the land, and
probably there were many little straw huts, little temporary houses, among the green corn : and fine roads,
such as the Etruscans taught the Romans to build,
went between the hills : and the high black walls, with
towers, wound along the hill-crest.

The Etruscans, though they grew rich as traders and metal-workers, seem to have lived chiefly by the land. The intense culture of the land by the Italian peasant of to-day seems like the remains of the Etruscan system. On the other hand, it was Roman, and not Etruscan, to have large villas in the country, with the great compound or " factory " for the slaves, who were shut in at night, and in gangs taken out to labour during the day. The huge farms of Sicily and Lombardy and other parts of Italy must be a remains of this Roman system: the big *fattorie*. But one imagines the Etruscans had a different system: that the peasants were serfs rather than slaves: that they had their own small portions of land, which they worked to full pitch, from father to son, giving a portion of the produce to the masters, keeping a portion for themselves. So they were half-free, at least, and had a true life of their own, stimulated by the religious life of their masters.

The Romans changed it all. They did not like the country. In palmy days they built great villas with barracks for slaves, out in the country. But, even so, it was easier to get rich by commerce or conquest. So the Romans gradually abandoned the land, which fell into neglect and prepared the way for the Dark Ages.

The wind blows stiffer and stiffer from the south-west. There are no trees: but even the bushes bend away from it. And when we get to the crown of the long, lonely hill on which stood the Etruscan Tarquinii we are almost blown from our feet, and have to sit down behind a thicket of bushes, for a moment's shelter: to watch the great black-and-white cattle stepping slowly down to the drinking-place, the young bulls curving and playing. All along the hilltop the green wheat ruffles like soft hair. Away inland the green land looks empty, save for a far-off town perched on a hilltop, like a vision. On the next hill, towards the sea, Tarquinia holds up her square towers, in vain.

And we are sitting on what would be the arx of the vanished city. Somewhere here the augurs held up their curved staffs, and watched the birds move across the quarters of the sky. We can do so much even to-day. But of the city I cannot find even one stone. It is so lonely and open.

One can go back up a different road, and in through another gate of the city of to-day. We drop quickly down, in the fierce wind, down to calm. The road winds up slowly from the little valley, but we are in shelter from the wind. So, we pass the first wall, through the first mediaeval gateway. The road winds inside the wall, past the *Dazio*, but there are no houses. A bunch of men are excitedly playing *morra*, and the shouts of the numbers come up like explosions, with wild excitement. The men glance at us apprehensively, but laugh as we laugh.

So we pass on through a second frowning gateway,

inside the second circle of walls. And still we are not in the town. There is still a third wall, and a third massive gate. And then we are in the old part of the town, where the graceful little palazzos of the Middle Ages are turned into stables and barns, and into houses for poor peasants. In front of the lower storey of one little old palace, now a blacksmith's shop, the smith is shoeing a refractory mule, which kicks and plunges, and brings loud shouts from the inevitable little group of onlookers.

Queer and lonely and slummy the waste corners and narrow streets seem, forlorn, as if belonging to another age. On a beautiful stone balcony a bit of poor washing is drying. The houses seem dark and furtive, people lurking like rats. And then again rises another tall, sharp-edged tower, blank and blind. They have a queer effect on a town, these sharp, rigid, blind, meaningless towers, soaring away with their sharp edges into the sky, for no reason, beyond the house-roofs; and from the far distance, when one sees the little city from far off, suggesting the factory chimneys of a modern town.

They are the towers which in the first place were built for retreat and defence, when this coast was ravaged by sea-rovers, Norman adventurers, or Barbary pirates that were such a scourge to the Mediterranean. Later, however, the mediaeval nobles built towers just for pure swank, to see who should have the tallest, till a town like Bologna must have bristled like a porcupine in a rage, or like Pittsburg with chimney-stacks—but square ones. Then the law forbade towers—and towers, after having scraped the heavens, began to come down. There are some still, however, in Tarquinia, where age overlaps age.

V
VULCI

V

ANCIENT ETRURIA consisted of a league, or loose religious Confederacy of twelve cities, each city embracing some miles of country all around, so that we may say there were twelve states, twelve city-states, the famous *dodecapolis* of the ancient world, the Latin *duodecim populi Etruriae*. Of these twelve city-states, Tarquinii was supposed to be the oldest, and the chief. Caere is another city: and not far off, to the north, Vulci.

Vulci is now called Volci—though there is no city, only a hunting-ground for treasure in Etruscan tombs. The Etruscan city fell into decay in the decline of the Roman Empire, and either lapsed owing to the malaria which came to fill this region with death, or else was finally wiped out, as Ducati says, by the Saracens. Anyhow there is no life there now.

I asked the German boy about the Etruscan places along the coast: Volci, Vetulonia, Populonia. His answer was always the same: "Nothing! Nothing! There is nothing there!"

However, we determined to look at Volci. It lies only about a dozen miles north of Tarquinia. We took the train, one station only, to Montalto di Castro, and were rattled up to the little town on the hill, not far inland.

141

The morning was still fairly early—and Saturday. But the town, or village, on the hill was very quiet and dead-alive. We got down from the bus in a sort of nowhere-seeming little piazza: the town had no centre of life. But there was a café, so in we went, asked for coffee, and where could we get a carriage to take us to Volci.

The man in the little café was yellow and slow, with the slow smile of the peasants. He seemed to have no energy at all: and eyed us lethargically. Probably he had malaria—though the fevers were not troubling him at the time. But it had eaten into his life.

He said, did we want to go to the bridge—the *Ponte*? I said yes, the *Ponte dell'Abbadia*: because I knew that Volci was near to this famous old bridge of the monastery. I asked him if we could get a light cart to drive us out. He said it would be difficult. I said, then we could walk: it was only five miles, eight kilometres. "Eight kilometres!" he said, in the slow, laconic malarial fashion, looking at me with a glint of ridicule in his black eyes. "It is at least twelve!"

"The book says eight!" I insisted stoutly. They always want to make distances twice as long, if you are to hire a carriage. But he watched me slowly, and shook his head. "Twelve!" he said. "Then we must have a carriage," said I. "You wouldn't find your way anyhow," said the man. "Is there a carriage?" He didn't know. There was one, but it had gone off somewhere this morning, and wouldn't be back till two or three in the afternoon. The usual story.

I insisted, was there no little cart, no *barrocino*, no *carretto*? He slowly shook his head. But I continued to insist, gazing at him fixedly, as if a carriage *must* be produced. So at last he went out, to look. He came back, after a time, shaking his head. Then he had a colloquy with his wife. Then he went out again, and was gone ten minutes.

A dusty little baker, a small man very full of energy, as little Italians often are, came in and asked for a drink. He sat down a minute and drank his drink, eyeing us from his floury face. Then he got up and left the shop again. In a moment the café man returned, and said that perhaps there was a *carretto*. I asked where it was. He said the man was coming.

The drive to the Ponte was apparently two hours— then the trip would be six hours. We should have to take a little food with us—there was nothing there.

A small-faced, weedy sort of youth appeared in the doorway: also malaria! We could have the *carretto*. "For how much?" "Seventy liras!" "Too much!" said I. "Far too much! Fifty, or nothing. Take it or leave it, fifty!" The youth in the doorway looked blank. The café man, always with his faint little sardonic smile, told the youth to go and ask. The youth went. We waited. Then the youth came back, to say all right! So! "How long?" "*Subito!*" *Subito* means immediately, but it is as well to be definite. "Ten minutes?" said I. "Perhaps twenty!" said the youth. "Better say twenty!" said the café man: who was an honest man, really, and rather pleasant in his silent way.

We went out to buy a little food, and the café man went with us. The shops in the place were just holes. We went to the baker. Outside stood a cart being loaded with bread, by the youth and the small, quicksilver baker. Inside the shop, we bought a long loaf, and a few bits of sliced sausage, and asked for cheese. There was no cheese—but they would get us some. We waited an infinite while. I said to the café man, who waited alongside, full of interest: "Won't the *carretto* be ready?" He turned round and pointed to the tall, randy mare between the shafts of the bread-cart outside. "That's the horse that will take you. When the bread is delivered, they will hitch her into the *carretto*, and the youth will drive you." There was nothing for it but patience, for the baker's mare and the baker's youth were our only hope. The cheese came at last. We wandered out to look for oranges. There was a woman selling them on a low bench beside the road, but B., who was getting impatient, didn't like the look of them. So we went across to a little hole of a shop where another woman had oranges. They were tiny ones, and B. was rejecting them with impatient scorn. But the woman insisted they were sweet, sweet as apples, and full of juice. We bought four: and I bought a *finocchio* for a salad. But she was right. The oranges were exquisite, when we came to eat them, and we wished we had ten.

On the whole, I think the people in Montalto are honest and rather attractive, but most of them slow and silent. It must be the malaria every time.

The café man asked if we would stay the night. We said, was there an inn? He said: "Oh yes, several!" I asked where, and he pointed up the street. "But," said I, "what do you want with several hotels here?" "For the agents who come to buy agricultural produce," he said. "Montalto is the centre of a great agricultural industry, and many agents come, many!" However, I decided that, if we could, we would leave in the evening. There was nothing in Montalto to keep us.

At last the *carretto* was ready: a roomy, two-wheeled gig hung rather low. We got in, behind the dark, mulberry mare, and the baker's youth, who certainly hadn't washed his face for some days, started us on the trip. He was in an agony of shyness, stupefied.

The town is left behind at once. The green land, with squares of leaden-dark olives planted in rows, slopes down to the railway line, which runs along the coast parallel with the ancient Via Aurelia. Beyond the railway is the flatness of the coastal strip, and the whitish emptiness of the sea's edge. It gives a great sense of nothingness, the sea down there.

The mulberry mare, lean and spare, reaches out and makes a good pace. But very soon we leave the road and are on a wide, wide trail of pinkish clayey earth, map entirely due of ruts. In parts the mud is still deep, water stands in the fathomless mud-holes. But fortunately, for a week it hasn't rained, so the road is passable; most of the ruts are dry, and the wide trail, wide as a desert road which has no confines, is not difficult, only jolty. We run the risk of having our necks jerked out of their sockets by the impatient, long-striding mare.

The boy is getting over his shyness, now he is warmed up to driving, and proves outspoken and straightforward. I said to him: "What a good thing the road is dry!" "If it had been fifteen days ago," he said, "you couldn't have passed." But in the late afternoon, when we were returning on the same road, and I said: "In bad wet weather we should have to come through here on horseback," he replied: "Even with the *carretto* you can get through." "Always?" said I. "Always!" said he.

And that was how he was. Possibility or impossibility was just a frame of mind with him.

We were on the Maremma, that flat, wide plain of the coast that has been water-logged for centuries, and one of the most abandoned, wildest parts of Italy. Under the Etruscans, apparently, it was an intensely fertile plain. But the Etruscans seem to have been very clever drainage-engineers; they drained the land so that it was a waving bed of wheat, with their methods of intensive peasant culture. Under the Romans, however, the elaborate system of canals and levels of water fell into decay, and gradually the streams threw their mud along the coast and choked themselves, then

soaked into the land and made marshes and vast
stagnant shallow pools where the mosquitoes bred
like fiends, millions hatching on a warm May day;
and with the mosquitoes came the malaria, called the
marsh fever in the old days. Already in late Roman
times this evil had fallen on the Etruscan plains and
on the Campagna of Rome. Then, apparently, the
land rose in level, the sea-strip was wider but even
more hollow than before, the marshes became deadly,
and human life departed or was destroyed, or lingered
on here and there.

In Etruscan days, no doubt, large tracts of this coast
were covered with pine-forest, as are the slopes of the
mountains that rise a few miles inland, and stretches
of the coast still, farther north. The pleasant *pineta*,
or open, sparse forest of umbrella-pines, once spread
on and on, with tall arbutus and heather covering the
earth from which the reddish trunks rose singly, as
from an endless moor, and tufts of arbutus and broom
making thickets. The pine-woods farther north are
still delightful, so silent and bosky, with the umbrella
roofs.

But the pine will not bear being soaked. So, as the
great pools and marshes spread, the trees of Etruscan
days fell for ever, and great treeless tracts appeared,
covered with an almost impenetrable low jungle of
bush and scrub and reeds, spreading for miles, and
quite manless. The arbutus, that is always glossy
green, and the myrtle, the mastic-tree, heaths, broom,

and other spiny, gummy, coarse moorland plants rose up in dense luxuriance, to have their tops bent and whipped off by the ever-whipping winds from the sea, so that there was a low, dark jungle of scrub, less than man-high, stretching in places from the mountains almost to the sea. And here the wild boar roamed in herds; foxes and wolves hunted the rabbits, the hares, the roebuck; the innumerable wild-fowl and the flamingos walked the sickly, stricken shores of the great pools and the sea.

So the Maremma country lay for centuries, with cleared tracts between, and districts a little elevated, and therefore rich in produce, but for the most part a wilderness, where the herdsmen pastured sheep, if possible, and the buffaloes roamed unherded. In 1828, however, the Grand-duke Leopold of Tuscany signed the decree for the reclaiming of the Maremma, and lately the Italian Government has achieved splendid results — great tracts of farmland added on to the country's resources, and new farms stuck up.

But still there are large tracts of moorland. We bowled along the grassy ruts, towards the distant mountains, and first all was wheat; then it was moorland, with great, grey-headed carrion-crows floating around in the bareness; then a little thicket of ilex-oak; then another patch of wheat; and then a desolate sort of farmhouse, that somehow reminded one of America, a rather dismal farm on the naked prairie, all alone.

The youth told me he had been for two years *guard-iano*, or herdsman, at this place. The large cattle were lingering around the naked house, within the wire enclosure. But there was a notice that the place was shut off, because of foot-and-mouth disease. The driver saluted a dismal woman and two children as he drove by.

We made a good pace. The driver, Luigi, told me his father had been also a *guardiano*, a herdsman, in this district, his five sons following him. The youth would look round, into the distance, with that keen, far-off look of men who have always lived wild and apart, and who are in their own country. He knew every sign. And he was so glad to get out again, out of Montalto.

The father, however, had died, a brother had married and lived in the family house, and Luigi had gone to help the baker in Montalto. But he was not happy: caged. He revived and became alert once more out in the Maremma spaces. He had lived more or less alone all his life—he was only eighteen—and loneliness, space, was precious to him, as it is to a moorland bird.

The great hooded crows floated round, and many big meadow-larks rose up from the moor. Save for this, everything to us was silent. Luigi said that now the hunting season was closed: but still, if he had a gun, he could take a shot at those hooded crows. It was obvious he was accustomed to have a gun in his hand when he was out in the long, hot, malarial days, mounted on a pony, watching the herds of cattle roving on the Maremma. Cattle do not take malaria.

I asked him about game. He said there was much in the foothills there. And he pointed away ahead, to where the mountains began to rise, six or eight miles away. Now so much of the Maremma itself is drained and cleared, the game is in the hills. His father used to accompany the hunters in winter: they still arrive in winter-time, the hunters in their hunting outfit, with dogs, and a great deal of fuss and paraphernalia, from Rome or from Florence. And still they catch the wild boar, the fox, the *capriolo*: which I suppose means the roedeer rather than the wild goat. But the boar is the *pièce de resistance*. You may see his bristling carcass in the market-place in Florence, now and again, in winter. But, like every other wild thing on earth, he is becoming scarcer and scarcer. Soon the only animals left will be tame ones: man the tamest and most swarming. Adieu even to Maremma.

"There!" said the boy. "There is the bridge of the monastery!" We looked into the shallow hollow of green land, and could just see a little, black sort of tower by some bushes, in the empty landscape. There was a long, straight ditch or canal, and digging evidently going on. It was the Government irrigation works.

We left the road and went bowling over rough grass, by tracts of poor-looking oats. Luigi said they would cut these oats for fodder. There was a scrap of a herdsman's house, and new wire fences along the embankment of the big irrigation canal. This was new to Luigi. He turned the mare uphill again, towards the house, and asked the urchin where he was to get through the wire fence. The urchin explained—Luigi had it in a moment. He was intelligent as a wild thing, out here in his own spaces.

"Five years ago," he said, "there was none of this" —and he pointed around. "No canal, no fences, no oats, no wheat. It was all *maremma*, moorland, with no life save the hooded crows, the cattle and the herdsmen. Now the cattle are all going—the herds are only remnants. And the ranch-houses are being abandoned." He pointed away to a large house some miles off, on the nearest hill-foot. "There, there are no more cattle, no more herdsmen. The steam-plough comes and ploughs the earth, the machinery sows and reaps the wheat and oats, the people of the Maremma, instead of being more, are fewer. The wheat grows by machinery."

We were on a sort of trail again, bowling down a slight incline towards a bushy hollow and a black old ruin with a tower. Soon we saw that in the hollow was a tree-filled ravine, quite deep. And over the ravine a queer bridge, curving up like a rainbow, and narrow and steep and fortified-seeming. It soared over the ravine in one high curve, the stony path nipped in like a gutter between its broken walls, and charging straight at the black lava front of the ruin opposite, which was once a castle of the frontier. The little river in the gully, the Fiora, formed the boundary between the Papal States and Tuscany, so the castle guarded the bridge.

We wanted to get down, but Luigi made us wait, while he ran ahead to negotiate. He came back, climbed in, and drove up between the walls of the bridge. It was just wide enough for the cart : just. The walls of the bridge seemed to touch us. It was like climbing up a sort of gutter. Far below, way down in a thicket of bushes, the river rushed—the Fiora, a mere torrent or rain-stream.

We drove over the bridge, and at the far end the lava wall of the monastery seemed to shut us back, the mare's nose almost touched it. The road, however, turned to the left under an arched gateway. Luigi edged the mare round cleverly. There was just room to get her round with the *carretto*, out of the mouth of the bridge and under the archway, scraping the wall of the castle.

So! We were through. We drove a few yards past the ruin, and got down on a grassy place over the ravine. It was a wonderfully romantic spot. The ancient bridge, built in the first place by the Etruscans of Vulci, of blocks of black *tufo*, goes up in the air like a black bubble, so round and strange. The little river is in the bushy cleft, a hundred feet below. The bridge is in the sky, like a black bubble, most strange and lonely, with the poignancy of perfect things long forgotten. It has, of course, been restored in Roman and mediaeval days. But essentially it is Etruscan, a beautiful Etruscan movement.

Pressing on to it, on this side, is the black building of the castle, mostly in ruins, with grass growing from the tops of the walls and from the black tower. Like the bridge, it is built of blocks of reddish black, spongy lava-stone, but its blocks are much squarer.

And all around is a peculiar emptiness. The castle is not entirely ruined. It is a sort of peasant farmstead. Luigi knows the people who live there. And across the stream there are patches of oats, and two or three cattle feeding, and two children. But all on this side, towards the mountains, is heathy, waste moorland, over which the trail goes towards the hills, and towards a great house among trees which we had seen from the distance. That is the *Badia*, or monastery, which gave the name to the bridge. But it has long been turned into a villa. The whole of this property belonged to Lucien Bonaparte, Prince of Cassino, brother of Napoleon. He lived here after the death of his brother, as an Italian prince. In 1828 some oxen ploughing the land near the castle suddenly went through the surface of the earth, and sank into a tomb, in which were broken vases. This at once led to excavations. It was the time when the "Grecian urn" was most popular. Lucien Bonaparte had no interest in vases. He hired an overseer to superintend the excavating, giving orders that every painted fragment must be saved, but that coarse ware must be smashed, to prevent the cheapening of the market. So that the work went savagely on, vases and basketfuls of broken pieces were harvested, the coarse, rough black Etruscan ware was smashed to pieces, as it was discovered, the overseer guarding the workmen with his gun over his knees. Dennis saw this still happening in 1846, when Lucien was dead. But the work was still going on, under the Princess's charge. And vainly Dennis asked the overseer to spare him some of the rough black ware. Not one! Smash they went to earth, while the overseer sat with his gun over his knees ready to shoot. But the bits of painted pottery were most skilfully fitted together, by the Princess's expert workmen, and she would sell some patera or amphora for a thousand crowns, which had been a handful of potsherds. The tombs were opened, rifled, and then filled in with earth again. All the landed proprietors with property in the neighbourhood carried on excavations, and endless treasure was exhumed. Within two months of the time when he started excavating, Lucien Bonaparte had got more than two thousand Etruscan objects out of tombs occupying a few acres of ground. That the Etruscans should have left fortunes to the Bonapartes seems an irony: but so it was. Vulci had mines indeed: but mostly of painted vases, those " brides of quietness " which had been only too much ravished. The tombs have little to show now.

We ate our food, the mare cropping the grass. And

I wondered, seeing youths on bicycles, four or five, come swooping down the trail across stream, out of emptiness, dismount and climb the high curve of the bridge, then disappear into the castle. From the mountains a man came riding on an ass: a pleasant young man in corduroy velveteens. He was riding without a saddle. He had a word with Luigi, in the low, secretive tones of the country, and went on towards the bridge. Then across, two men on mules came trotting down to the bridge: and a peasant drove in two bullocks, whose horns pricked the sky from the tall poise of the bridge.

The place seemed very populous for so lonely a spot. And still, all the air was heavy with isolation, suspicion, guardedness. It was like being in the Middle Ages. I asked Luigi to go to the house for some wine. He said he didn't know if he could get it: but he went off, with the semi-barbaric reluctance and fear of approaching a strange place.

After a while he came back, to say the *dispensa* was shut, and he couldn't get any. "Then," said I, "let us go to the tombs! Do you know where they are?" He pointed vaguely into the distance of the moorland, and said they were there, but that we should want candles. The tombs were dark, and no one was there. "Then let us get candles from the peasants," I said. He answered again, the *dispensa* was shut, and we couldn't get candles. He seemed uneasy and de- pressed, as the people always are when there is a little difficulty. They are so afraid and mistrustful of one another.

We walked back to the black ruin, through a dark gateway that had been portcullised, into a half-ruined black courtyard, curiously gloomy. And here seven or eight men were squatting or standing about, their shiny bicycles leaning against the ruined walls. They were queer-looking men, youngish fellows, smallish, unshaven, dirty; not peasants, but workmen of some sort, who looked as if they had been swept together among the rubbish. Luigi was evidently nervous of them: not that they were villains, merely he didn't know them. And he had one friend among them: a queer young fellow of about twenty, in a close-fitting blue jersey, a black, black beard on his rather delicate but *gamin* face, and an odd sort of smile. This young fellow came roving round us, with a queer, uneasy, half-smiling curiosity. The men all seemed like that, uneasy and as it were outcast, but with an unknown quality too. They were, in reality, the queer, poorest sort of natives of this part of the Maremma.

The courtyard of the castle was black and sinister, yet very interesting in its ruined condition. There were a few forlorn rat-like signs of peasant farming. And an outside staircase, once rather grand, went up to what was now apparently the inhabited quarter, two or three rooms facing the bridge.

The feeling of suspicion and almost of opposition, negative rather than active, was still so strong we went out again and on to the bridge. Luigi, in a dilemma, talked mutteringly to his black-bearded young friend with the bright eyes: all the men seemed to have queer, quick, bright black eyes, with a glint on them such as a mouse's eyes have.

At last I asked him, flatly: "Who are all those men?" He muttered that they were the workmen and navvies. I was puzzled to know *what* workmen and navvies, in this loneliness? Then he explained they were working on the irrigation works, and had come in to the *dispensa* for their wages and to buy things—it was Saturday afternoon—but that the overseer, who kept the *dispensa*, and who sold wine and necessaries to the workmen, hadn't come yet to open the place, so we couldn't get anything.

At least, Luigi didn't explain all this. But when he said these were the workmen from the irrigation diggings, I understood it all.

By this time, we and our desire for candles had become a feature in the landscape. I said to Luigi, why didn't he ask the *peasants*. He said they hadn't any. Fortunately at that moment an unwashed woman appeared at an upper window in the black wall. I asked her if she couldn't sell us a candle. She retired to think about it—then came back to say, surlily, it would be sixty centimes. I threw her a lira, and she dropped a candle. So!

Then the black-bearded young fellow glintingly said we should want more than one candle. So I asked

the woman for another, and threw her fifty centimes—
as she was contemplating giving me the change for
the lira. She dropped another candle.

B. and I moved towards the *carretto*, with Luigi.
But I could see he was still unhappy. "Do you
know where the tombs are?" I asked him. Again he
waved vaguely: "Over there!" But he was unhappy.
"Would it be better to take one of those men for
a guide?" I said to him. And I got the inevitable
answer: "It is as you think." "If *you* don't know
the tombs well," I said to him, "then find a man to
come with us." He still hesitated, with that dumb
uncertainty of these people. "Find a man anyhow,"
I said, and off he went, feebly.

He came back in relief with the peasant, a short
but strong *maremmano* of about forty, unshaven but
not unclean. His name was Marco, and he had put on
his best jacket to accompany us. He was quiet and
determined-seeming—a brownish blond, not one of
the queer black natives with the queer round soft
contours. His boy of about thirteen came with him,
and they two climbed on to the back of the *carretto*.

Marco gave directions, and we bowled down the
trail, then away over a slight track, on to the heathy
strong moorland. After us came a little black-eyed
fellow on a bicycle. We passed on the left a small
encampment of temporary huts made of planks, with
women coming out to look. By the trail were huge
sacks of charcoal, and the black charcoal-burners, just

down from the mountains, for the week-end, stood aside to look at us. The asses and mules stood drooping.

This was the winter camp of the charcoal-burners. In a week or so, Marco told me, they would abandon this camp and go up into the mountains, out of reach of the fevers which begin in May. Certainly they looked a vigorous bunch, if a little wild. I asked Marco if there was much fever—meaning malaria. He said: "Not much." I asked him if he had had any attacks. He said: "No, never." It is true he looked broad and healthy, with a queer, subdued, explosive sort of energy. Yet there was a certain motionless, rather worn look in his face, a certain endurance and sallowness, which seemed like malaria to me. I asked Luigi, our driver, if he had had any fever. At first he too said no. Then he admitted he had had a touch now and then. Which was evident, for his face was small and yellowish, evidently the thing had eaten into him. Yet he too, like Marco, had a strong, *manly* energy, more than the ordinary Italians. It is evidently the thing, in these parts, to deny that the malaria has ever touched you.

To the left, out of the heath, rose great flattish mounds, great tumuli, bigger than those of Cerveteri. I asked Marco were those the tombs? He said those were the tumuli, Coccumella and Coccumelletta—but that we would go first to the river tombs.

We were descending a rocky slope towards the brink of the ravine, which was full of trees, as ever.

Far away, apparently, behind us to the right, stood
the lonely black tower of the castle, across the moorland
whence we had come. Across the ravine was a long,
low hill, grassy and moorland: and farther down the
stream were the irrigation works. The country was
all empty and abandoned-seeming, yet with that
peculiar, almost ominous, poignancy of places where
life has once been intense. "Where do they say the
city of Vulci was?" I asked Marco. He pointed across
stream, to the long, low elevation along the opposite
side of the ravine. I guessed it had been there—since
the tombs were on this side. But it looked very low
and undefended, for an Etruscan site: so open to the
world! I supposed it had depended upon its walls,
seawards, and the ravine inland. I asked Marco if
anything was there; some sign of where the walls had
gone round. He said: "Nothing!" It has evidently
not been a very large city, like Caere and Tarquinia.
But it was one of the cities of the League, and very
rich indeed, judging from the thousands of painted
vases which have been found in the tombs here.

The rocky descent was too uneven. We got out of
the cart, and went on foot. Luigi left the mare, and
Marco led us on, down to a barb-wire fence. We should
never, never have found the place ourselves. Marco
expertly held the wire apart, and we scrambled through
on to the bushy, rocky side of the ravine. The trees
rose from the riverside, some leaves bright green.
And we descended a rough path, past the entrance-

passage to a tomb most carefully locked with an iron
gate, and defended with barbed wire, like a hermit's
cave with the rank vegetation growing up to choke it
again.

Winding among rank vegetation and fallen rocks
of the face of the ravine, we came to the openings of
the tombs, which were cut into the face of the rock,
and must have been a fine row once, like a row of rock-
houses with a pleasant road outside, along the ravine.
But now they are gloomy holes down which one must
clamber through the excavated earth. Once inside,
with the three candles—for the black-faced youth on
the bicycle had brought a stump too—we were in
gloomy wolves' dens of places, with large chambers
opening off one another as at Cerveteri, damp beds of
rock for the coffins, and huge grisly stone coffins,
seven feet long, lying in disorder, among fallen rocks
and rubble, in some of them the bones and man-dust
still lying dismally. There was nothing to see but
these black, damp chambers, sometimes cleared, sometimes with coarse great sarcophagi and broken rubbish
and excavation-rubble left behind in the damp, grisly
darkness.

Sometimes we had to wriggle into the tombs on our
bellies, over the mounds of rubble, going down into
holes like rats, while the bats flew blindly in our faces.
Once inside, we clambered in the faint darkness over
huge pieces of rock and broken stone, from dark
chamber to chamber, four or five or even more chambers

to a tomb, all cut out of the rock and made to look like houses, with the sloping roof-tilts and the central roof-beam. From these roofs hung clusters of pale brown furry bats, in bunches, like bunches of huge furry hops. One could hardly believe they were alive, till I saw the squat little fellow of the bicycle holding his candle up to one of the bunches, singeing the bats' hair, burning the torpid creatures, so the skinny wings began to flutter, and half-stupefied, half-dead bats fell from the clusters of the roof, then groped on the wing and began to fly low, staggering towards the outlet. The dark little fellow took pleasure in burning them. But I stopped him at it, and he was afraid, and left them alone.

He was a queer fellow—quite short, with the fat, soft, round curves, and black hair and sallow face and black bats' eyes of a certain type of this district. He was perhaps twenty years old, and like a queer burrowing dumb animal. He would creep into holes in the queerest way, with his queer, soft, round hind-quarters jutting behind : just like some uncanny animal. And I noticed the backs of his ears were all scaly and raw with sores ; whether from dirt or some queer disease, who can say. He seemed healthy and alive enough, otherwise. And he seemed quite unconscious of his sore ears, with an animal unconsciousness.

Marco, who was a much higher type, knew his way about, and led us groping and wriggling and clamber-ing from tomb to tomb, among the darkness and

brokenness and bats and damp, then out among the
fennel and bushes of the ravine top, then in again into
some hole. He showed us a tomb whence only last year
they had taken a big stone statue—he showed me where
it had stood, there, in the innermost chamber, with its
back to the wall. And he told me of all the vases,
mostly broken pieces, that he too had lifted from the
dirt, on the stone beds.

But now there is nothing, and I was tired of climbing
into these gruesome holes, one after another, full of
damp and great fallen rocks. Nothing living or beautiful is left behind—nothing. I was glad when we came
to the end of the excavated tombs, and saw beyond
only the ravine bank grown over with bushes and
fennel and great weeds. Probably many a vase and
many a stone coffin still lie hidden there—but let
them lie.

We went back along the path the way we had come,
to climb back to the upper level. As we came to the
gangway leading to the locked tomb Marco told me
that in here were paintings and some things left behind. Probably it was the famous François tomb with
the paintings that are copied in the Vatican museum.
It was opened by the excavator François in 1857, and is
one of the very, very few painted tombs found at Vulci.

We tried in vain to get in. Short of smashing the
lock, it was impossible. Of course, in these expeditions,
one should arm oneself with official permits. But it
means having officials hanging round.

So we climbed up to the open world, and Luigi made us get into the *carretto*. The mare pulled us jolting across towards the great tumuli, which we wanted to see. They are huge grassy-bushy mounds, like round, low hills. The band of stonework round the base, if it be there, is buried.

Marco led us inside the dense passage of brambles and bushes which leads to the opening into the tumulus. Already this passage is almost blocked up, overgrown. One has to crawl under the scratching brambles, like a rabbit.

And at last one is in the plain doorway of the tumulus itself. Here, even in 1829, two weird stone sphinxes guarded the entrance. Now there is nothing. And inside the passage or at the angles were lions and griffins on guard. What now shall we find as we follow the candlelight in the narrow, winding passage? It is like being in a mine, narrow passages winding on and on, from nowhere to nowhere. We had not any great length of candle left: four stumps. Marco left one stump burning at the junction of the passages as a signpost, and on and on we went, from nowhere to nowhere, stooping a little, our hats brushing the clusters of bats that hung from the ceiling as we went on, one after the other, pinned all the time in the narrow stone corridors that never led anywhere or did anything. Sometimes there was a niche in the wall—that was all.

There must, surely, be a central burial chamber, to

which the passages finally lead. But we didn't find it. And Marco said there was no such thing—the tumulus was all passages and nothing but passages. But Dennis says that when the tumulus was opened in 1829 there were two small chambers in the heart of the mound, and rising from these, two shafts of masonry which passed up to the apex of the mound, and probably these supported great monuments, probably the phallic cippi. On the floor of the chamber were fragments of bronze and frail gold. But now there is nothing; the centre of the tumulus is no doubt collapsed.

It was like being burrowing inside some ancient pyramid. This was quite unlike any other Etruscan tomb we had seen: and if this tumulus was a tomb, then it must have been a very important person whose coffin formed the nut inside all this shell—a person important as a Pharaoh, surely. The Etruscans were queer people, and this tumulus, with no peripheral tombs, only endless winding passages, must be either a reminiscence of prehistoric days or of Egyptian pyramids.

When we had had enough of running along passages in nowhere we got out, scrambled through the bramble tangle, and were thankful to see clear heaven again. We all piled into the *carretto*, and the mare nobly hauled us up to the trail. The little dark fellow sailed ahead silently, on his bicycle, to open the gate for us. We looked round once more at the vast mound of the

Coccumella, which strange dead hands piled in soft
earth over two tiny death-chambers, so long ago: and
even now it is weirdly conspicuous across the flat
Maremma. A strange, strange nut indeed, with a
kernel of perpetual mystery! And once it rose suave
as a great breast, tipped with the budded monuments
of the cippi! It is too problematic. We turn our back
on it all as the *carretto* jolts over the tomb-rifled earth.
There is something gloomy, if rather wonderful, about
Vulci.

The charcoal-burners were preparing to wash their
faces for Sunday, in the little camp. The women stood
smiling as we drove by on the moor. "Oh, how fat
thou hast got!" Luigi shouted to one plump and
smiling woman. "*You* haven't though!" she shouted
back at him. "*Tu pure no!*"

At the bridge we said good-bye to Marco and his
boy, then we pulled over the arch once more. But on
the other side Luigi wanted to drink. So he and I
scrambled down to the spring, the old, thin-trickling
spring, and drank cool water. The river rushed below:
the bridge arched its black, soaring rainbow above,
and we heard the shouts of mule-drivers driving the
mules over the arch.

Once this old bridge carried an aqueduct, and it is
curious to see the great stalactitic mass that hangs like
a beard down the side facing the mountains. But the
aqueduct is gone, the muddy stalactitic mass itself is
crumbling. Everything passes!

So we climbed up and into the *carretto*, and away went the mare at a spanking pace. We passed the young man in velveteens, on the donkey—a peasant from the hills, Luigi said he was. And we met horsemen riding towards us, towards the hills, away from Montalto. It was Saturday afternoon, with a bright sea-wind blowing strong over the Maremma, and men travelling away from work, on horseback, on mules, or on asses. And some drove laden donkeys out to the hills.

" It would be a good life," I said to Luigi, " to live here, and have a house on the hills, and a horse to ride, and space: except for the malaria ! "

Then, having previously confessed to me that the malaria was still pretty bad, though children often escaped it, but grown people rarely; the fever inevitably came to shake them sometimes; that Montalto was more stricken than the open country; and that in the time of rains the roads were impassable—one was cut off—now Luigi changed his tune: said there was almost no fever any more; the roads were always passable; in Montalto people came at bathing season to bathe in the sea, having little cane huts on the coast: the roads were always easily passable, easily ! and that you never got fever at all if you were properly fed, and had a bit of meat now and then, and a decent glass of wine. He wanted me so much to come and have some abandoned house in the foothills; and he would look after my horses, and we would go hunting together—even out of season, for there was no one to catch you.

B. dozed lightly while we drove joltingly on. It was a dream too. I would like it well enough—if I were convinced about that malaria. And I would certainly have Luigi to look after the horses. He hasn't a grand appearance, but he is solitary and courageous and surely honest, solitary, and far more manly than the townsmen or the grubb'ng peasants.

So, we have seen all we could see of Vulci. If we want to see what the Etruscans buried there we must go to the Vatican, or to the Florence museum, or to the British Museum in London, and see vases and statues, bronzes, sarcophagi and jewels. In the British Museum lie the contents, for the most part, of the famous Tomb of Isis, where lay buried a lady whom Dennis thought was surely Egyptian, judging from her statue, that is stiff and straight, and from the statuette of " Isis," the six ostrich eggs and other imported things that went to the grave with her: for in death she must be what she was in life, as exactly as possible. This was the Etruscan creed. How the Egyptian lady came to Vulci, and how she came to be buried there along with a lady of ancient Etruria, down in that bit of the Vulci necropolis now called Polledrara, who knows? But all that is left of her is now in the British Museum. Vulci has nothing. Anyhow she was surely not Egyptian at all. Anything of the archaic east Mediterranean seemed to Dennis Egyptian.

So it is. The site of Vulci was lost from Roman times till 1828. Once found, however, the tombs were rapidly gutted by the owners, everything precious was taken away, then the tombs were either closed again or abandoned. All the thousands of vases that the Etruscans gathered so lovingly and laid by their dead, where are they? Many are still in existence. But they are everywhere except at Vulci.

VI
VOLTERRA

VI

VOLTERRA is the most northerly of the great Etruscan cities of the west. It lies back some thirty miles from the sea, on a towering great bluff of rock that gets all the winds and sees all the world, looking out down the valley of the Cecina to the sea, south over vale and high land to the tips of Elba, north to the imminent mountains of Carrara, inward over the wide hills of the Pre-Apennines, to the heart of Tuscany.

You leave the Rome-Pisa train at Cecina, and slowly wind up the valley of the stream of that name, a green, romantic, forgotten sort of valley, in spite of all the come-and-go of ancient Etruscans and Romans, mediaeval Volterrans and Pisans, and modern traffic. But the traffic is not heavy. Volterra is a sort of inland island, still curiously isolated, and grim.

The small, forlorn little train comes to a stop at the Saline di Volterra, the famous old salt works now belonging to the State, where brine is pumped out of deep wells. What passengers remain in the train are transferred to one old little coach across the platform, and at length this coach starts to creep like a beetle up the slope, up a cog-and-ratchet line, shoved by a small engine behind. Up the steep but round slope among

173

the vineyards and olives you pass almost at walking-pace, and there is not a flower to be seen, only the beans make a whiff of perfume now and then, on the chill air, as you rise and rise, above the valley below, coming level with the high hills to south, and the bluff of rock with its two or three towers, ahead.

After a certain amount of backing and changing, the fragment of a train eases up at a bit of a cold wayside station, and is finished. The world lies below. You get out, transfer yourself to a small ancient motor-omnibus, and are rattled up to the final level of the city, into a cold and gloomy little square, where the hotel is.

The hotel is simple and somewhat rough, but quite friendly, pleasant in its haphazard way. And what is more, it has central heating, and the heat is on, this cold, almost icy, April afternoon. Volterra lies only 1800 feet above the sea, but it is right in the wind, and cold as any alp.

The day was Sunday, and there was a sense of excitement and fussing, and a bustling in and out of temporarily important persons, and altogether a smell of politics in the air. The waiter brought us tea, of a sort, and I asked him what was doing. He replied that a great banquet was to be given this evening to the new *podestà* who had come from Florence to govern the city, under the new regime. And evidently he felt that this was such a hugely important " party " occasion we poor outsiders were of no account.

It was a cold, grey afternoon, with winds round the hard dark corners of the hard, narrow mediaeval town, and crowds of black-dressed, rather squat little men and pseudo-elegant young women pushing and loitering in the streets, and altogether that sense of furtive grinning and jeering and threatening which always accompanies a public occasion—a political one especially —in Italy, in the more out-of-the-way centres. It is as if the people, alabaster-workers and a few peasants, were not sure which side they wanted to be on, and therefore were all the more ready to exterminate anyone who was on the other side. This fundamental uneasiness, indecision, is most curious in the Italian soul. It is as if the people could never be wholeheartedly anything: because they can't trust anything. And this inability to trust is at the root of the political extravagance and frenzy. They don't trust themselves, so how can they trust their " leaders " or their " party "?

Volterra, standing sombre and chilly alone on her rock, has always, from Etruscan days on, been grimly jealous of her own independence. Especially she has struggled against the Florentine yoke. So what her actual feelings are, about this new-old sort of village tyrant, the *podestà*, whom she is banqueting this evening, it would be hard, probably, even for the Volterrans themselves to say. Anyhow the cheeky girls salute one with the " Roman " salute, out of sheer effrontery: a salute which has nothing to do with me, so I don't return it. Politics of all sorts are anathema. But in an Etruscan city which held out so long against Rome I consider the Roman salute unbecoming, and the Roman *imperium* unmentionable.

It is amusing to see on the walls, too, chalked fiercely up: *Morte a Lenin!* though that poor gentleman has been long enough dead, surely, even for a Volterran to have heard of it. And more amusing still is the legend permanently painted: *Mussolini ha sempre ragione!* Some are born infallible, some achieve infallibility, and some have it thrust upon them.

But it is not for me to put even my little finger in any political pie. I am sure every post-war country has hard enough work to get itself governed, without outsiders interfering or commenting. Let those rule who can rule.

We wander on, a little dismally, looking at the stony stoniness of the mediaeval town. Perhaps on a warm sunny day it might be pleasant, when shadow was attractive and a breeze welcome. But on a cold, grey, windy afternoon of April, Sunday, always especially dismal, with all the people in the streets, bored and uneasy, and the stone buildings peculiarly sombre and hard and resistant, it is no fun. I don't care about the bleak but truly mediaeval piazza: I don't care if the Palazzo Pubblico has all sorts of amusing coats of arms on it: I don't care about the cold cathedral, though it is rather nice really, with a glow of dusky

candles and a smell of Sunday incense: I am disappointed in the wooden sculpture of the taking down
of Jesus, and the bas-reliefs don't interest me. In
short, I am hard to please.

The modern town is not very large. We went down
a long, stony street, and out of the Porta dell' Arco, the
famous old Etruscan gate. It is a deep old gateway,
almost a tunnel, with the outer arch facing the desolate
country on the skew, built at an angle to the old road,
to catch the approaching enemy on his right side,
where the shield did not cover him. Up handsome
and round goes the arch, at a good height, and with
that peculiar weighty richness of ancient things; and
three dark heads, now worn featureless, reach out
curiously and inquiringly, one from the keystone of
the arch, one from each of the arch bases, to gaze
from the city and into the steep hollow of the world
beyond.

Strange, dark old Etruscan heads of the city gate,
even now they are featureless they still have a peculiar,
out-reaching life of their own. Ducati says they represented the heads of slain enemies hung at the city
gate. But they don't hang. They stretch with curious
eagerness forward. Nonsense about dead heads. They
were city deities of some sort.

And the archaeologists say that only the doorposts
of the outer arch, and the inner walls, are Etruscan
work. The Romans restored the arch, and set the
heads back in their old positions. (Unlike the Romans

to set anything back in its old position!) While the wall above the arch is merely mediæval.

But we'll call it Etruscan still. The roots of the gate, and the dark heads, these they cannot take away from the Etruscans. And the heads are still on the watch.

The land falls away steeply, across the road in front of the arch. The road itself turns east, under the walls of the modern city, above the world: and the sides of the road, as usual outside the gates, are dump-heaps, dump-heaps of plaster and rubble, dump-heaps of the white powder from the alabaster works, the waste edge of the town.

The path turns away from under the city wall, and dips down along the brow of the hill. To the right we can see the tower of the church of Santa Chiara, standing on a little platform of the irregularly-dropping hill. And we are going there. So we dip downwards above a Dantesque, desolate world, down to Santa Chiara, and beyond. Here the path follows the top of what remains of the old Etruscan wall. On the right are little olive-gardens and bits of wheat. Away beyond is the dismal sort of crest of modern Volterra. We walk along, past the few flowers and the thick ivy, and the bushes of broom and marjoram, on what was once the Etruscan wall, far out from the present city wall. On the left the land drops steeply, in uneven and unhappy descents.

The great hilltop or headland on which Etruscan "Volterra," *Velathri*, *Vlathri*, once stood spreads out

jaggedly, with deep-cleft valleys in between, more or
less in view, spreading two or three miles away. It is
something like a hand, the bluff steep of the palm
sweeping in a great curve on the east and south, to
seawards, the peninsulas or fingers running jaggedly
inland. And the great wall of the Etruscan city swept
round the south and eastern bluff, on the crest of
steeps and cliffs, turned north and crossed the first
finger, or peninsula, then started up hill and down
dale over the fingers and into the declivities, a wild
and fierce sort of way, hemming in the great crest.
The modern town occupies merely the highest bit of
the Etruscan city site.

The walls themselves are not much to look at, when
you climb down. They are only fragments, now, huge
fragments of embankment, rather than wall, built of
uncemented square masonry, in the grim, sad sort of
stone. One only feels, for some reason, depressed.
And it is pleasant to look at the lover and his lass
going along the top of the ramparts, which are now
olive-orchards, away from the town. At least they are
alive and cheerful and quick.

On from Santa Chiara the road takes us through
the grim and depressing little suburb-hamlet of San
Giusto, a black street that emerges upon the waste
open place where the church of San Giusto rises like
a huge and astonishing barn. It is so tall, the interior
should be impressive. But no! It is merely nothing.
The architects have achieved nothing, with all that

tallness. The children play around with loud yells and ferocity. It is Sunday evening, near sundown, and cold.

Beyond this monument of Christian dreariness we come to the Etruscan walls again, and what was evidently once an Etruscan gate: a dip in the wall-bank, with the groove of an old road running to it.

Here we sit on the ancient heaps of masonry and look into weird yawning gulfs, like vast quarries. The swallows, turning their blue backs, skim away from the ancient lips and over the really dizzy depths, in the yellow light of evening, catching the upward gusts of wind, and flickering aside like lost fragments of life, truly frightening above those ghastly hollows. The lower depths are dark grey, ashy in colour, and in part wet, and the whole thing looks new, as if it were some enormous quarry all slipping down.

This place is called *Le Balze*—the cliffs. Apparently the waters which fall on the heights of Volterra collect in part underneath the deep hill and wear away at some places the lower strata, so that the earth falls in immense collapses. Across the gulf, away from the town, stands a big, old, picturesque, isolated building, the *Badia* or Monastery of the Camaldolesi, sad-looking, destined at last to be devoured by *Le Balze*, its old walls already splitting and yielding.

From time to time, going up to the town homewards, we come to the edge of the walls and look out into the vast glow of gold, which is sunset, marvellous,

the steep ravines sinking in darkness, the farther
valley silently, greenly gold, with hills breathing
luminously up, passing out into the pure, sheer gold
gleams of the far-off sea, in which a shadow, perhaps
an island, moves like a mote of life. And like great
guardians the Carrara mountains jut forward, naked
in the pure light like flesh, with their crests portentous : so that they seem to be advancing on us :
while all the vast concavity of the west roars with gold
liquescency, as if the last hour had come, and the
gods were smelting us all back into yellow transmuted
oneness.

But nothing is being transmuted. We turn our
faces, a little frightened, from the vast blaze of gold,
and in the dark, hard streets the town band is just
chirping up, brassily out of tune as usual, and the
populace, with some maidens in white, are streaming
in crowds towards the piazza. And, like the band, the
populace also is out of tune, buzzing with the inevitable suppressed jeering. But they are going to form
a procession.

When we come to the square in front of the hotel,
and look out from the edge into the hollow world of
the west, the light is sunk red, redness gleams up
from the far-off sea below, pure and fierce, and the
hollow places in between are dark. Over all the world
is a low red glint. But only the town, with its narrow
streets and electric light, is impervious.

The banquet, apparently, was not till nine o'clock,

and all was hubbub. B. and I dined alone soon after seven, like two orphans whom the waiters managed to remember in between whiles. They were so thrilled getting all the glasses and goblets and decanters, hundreds of them, it seemed, out of the big chiffonnier-cupboard that occupied the back of the dining-room, and whirling them away, stacks of glittering glass, to the banquet-room : while out-of-work young men would poke their heads in through the doorway, black hats on, overcoats hung over one shoulder, and gaze with bright inquiry through the room, as though they expected to see Lazarus risen, and not seeing him, would depart again to the nowhere whence they came. A banquet is a banquet, even if it is given to the devil himself; and the *podestà* may be an angel of light.

Outside was cold and dark. In the distance the town band tooted spasmodically, as if it were short-winded this chilly Sunday evening. And we, not bidden to the feast, went to bed. To be awakened occasionally by sudden and roaring noises—perhaps applause—and the loud and unmistakable howling of a child, well after midnight.

Morning was cold and grey again, with a chilly and forbidding country yawning and gaping and lapsing away beneath us. The sea was invisible. We walked the narrow cold streets, whose high, cold, dark stone walls seemed almost to press together, and we looked in at the alabaster workshops, where workmen, in

Monday-morning gloom and half-awakedness, were turning the soft alabaster, or cutting it out, or polishing it.

Everybody knows Volterra marble—so called—nowadays, because of the translucent bowls of it which hang under the electric lights, as shades, in half the hotels of the world. It is nearly as transparent as alum, and nearly as soft. They peel it down as if it were soap, and tint it pink or amber or blue, and turn it into all those things one does not want: tinted alabaster lamp-shades, light-bowls, statues, tinted or untinted, vases, bowls with doves on the rim, or vine-leaves, and similar curios. The trade seems to be going strong. Perhaps it is the electric-light demand: perhaps there is a revival of interest in "statuary." Anyhow there is no love lost between a Volterran alabaster worker and the lump of pale Volterran earth he turns into marketable form. Alas for the goddess of sculptured form, she has gone from here also.

But it is the old alabaster jars we want to see, not the new. As we hurry down the stony street the rain, icy cold, begins to fall. We flee through the glass doors of the museum, which has just opened, and which seems as if the alabaster inside had to be kept at a low temperature, for the place is dead-cold as a refrigerator.

Cold, silent, empty, unhappy the museum seems. But at last an old and dazed man arrives, in uniform, and asks quite scared what we want. "Why, to see the museum!" "*Ah! Ah! Ah si—si!*" It just dawns upon him that the museum is there to be looked at. "*Ah si, si, Signori !*"

We pay our tickets, and start in. It is really a very attractive and pleasant museum, but we had struck such a bitter cold April morning, with icy rain falling in the courtyard, that I felt as near to being in the tomb as I have ever done. Yet very soon, in the rooms with all those hundreds of little sarcophagi, ash-coffins, or urns, as they are called, the strength of the old life began to warm one up.

Urn is not a good word, because it suggests, to me at least, a vase, an amphora, a round and shapely jar : perhaps through association with Keats' *Ode to a Grecian Urn*—which vessel no doubt wasn't an urn at all, but a wine-jar—and with the " tea-urn " of children's parties. These Volterran urns, though correctly enough used for storing the ashes of the dead, are not round, they are not jars, they are small alabaster sarcophagi. And they are a peculiarity of Volterra. Probably because the Volterrans had the alabaster to hand.

Anyhow here you have them in hundreds, and they are curiously alive and attractive. They are not considered very highly as " art." One of the latest Italian writers on Etruscan things, Ducati, says : " If they have small interest from the artistic point of view, they are extremely valuable for the scenes they represent, either mythological or relative to the beliefs in the after-life."

George Dennis, however, though he too does not find much " art " in Etruscan things, says of the Volterran ash-chests : " The touches of Nature on these Etruscan urns, so simply but eloquently expressed, must appeal to the sympathies of all—they are chords to which every heart must respond; and I envy not the man who can walk through this museum unmoved, without feeling a tear rise to his eye,

> ' And recognizing ever and anon
> The breeze of Nature stirring in his soul.' "

The breeze of Nature no longer shakes dewdrops from our eyes, at least so readily, but Dennis is more alive than Ducati to that which is alive. What men mean nowadays by " art " it would be hard to say. Even Dennis said that the Etruscans never approached the pure, the sublime, the perfect beauty which Flaxman reached. To-day, this makes us laugh : the Greekified illustrator of Pope's *Homer* ! But the same instinct lies at the back of our idea of " art " still. Art is still to us something which has been well cooked—like a plate of spaghetti. An ear of wheat is not yet " art." Wait, wait till it has been turned into pure, into perfect macaroni.

For me, I get more real pleasure out of these Volterran ash-chests than out of—I had almost said, the Parthenon frieze. One wearies of the aesthetic quality —a quality which takes the edge off everything, and makes it seem " boiled down." A great deal of pure

Greek beauty has this boiled-down effect. It is too
much cooked in the artistic consciousness.

In Dennis' day a broken Greek or Greekish amphora
would fetch thousands of crowns in the market, if it
was the right " period," etc. These Volterran urns
fetched hardly anything. Which is a mercy, or they
would be scattered to the ends of the earth.

As it is, they are fascinating, like an open book of
life, and one has no sense of weariness with them,
though there are so many. They warm one up, like
being in the midst of life.

The downstairs rooms of ash-chests contain those
urns representing " Etruscan " subjects : those of sea-
monsters, the sea-man with fish-tail, and with wings,
the sea-woman the same : or the man with serpent-legs,
and wings, or the woman the same. It was Etruscan
to give these creatures wings, not Greek.

If we remember that in the old world the centre of
all power was at the depths of the earth, and at the
depths of the sea, while the sun was only a moving
subsidiary body : and that the serpent represented the
vivid powers of the inner earth, not only such powers
as volcanic and earthquake, but the quick powers that
run up the roots of plants and establish the great body
of the tree, the tree of life, and run up the feet and legs
of man, to establish the heart : while the fish was the
symbol of the depths of the waters, whence even light
is born : we shall see the ancient power these symbols
had over the imagination of the Volterrans. They were

a people faced with the sea, and living in a volcanic country.

Then the powers of the earth and the powers of the sea take life as they give life. They have their terrific as well as their prolific aspect.

Someone says the wings of the water-deities represent evaporation towards the sun, and the curving tails of the dolphin represent torrents. This is part of the great and controlling ancient idea of the come-and-go of the life-powers, the surging up, in a flutter of leaves and a radiation of wings, and the surging back, in torrents and waves and the eternal downpour of death.

Other common symbolic animals in Volterra are the beaked griffins, the creatures of the powers that tear asunder and, at the same time, are guardians of the treasure. They are lion and eagle combined, of the sky and of the earth with caverns. They do not allow the treasure of life, the gold, which we should perhaps translate as consciousness, to be stolen by thieves of life. They are guardians of the treasure: and then, they are the tearers asunder of those who must depart from life.

It is these creatures, creatures of the elements, which carry men away into death, over the border between the elements. So is the dolphin, sometimes: and so the hippocampus, the sea-horse; and so the centaur.

The horse is always the symbol of the strong animal

life of man : and sometimes he rises, a sea-horse, from the ocean : and sometimes he is a land creature, and half-man. And so he occurs on the tombs, as the passion in man returning into the sea, the soul retreating into the death-world at the depths of the waters : or sometimes he is a centaur, sometimes a female centaur, sometimes clothed in a lion-skin, to show his dread aspect, bearing the soul back, away, off into the otherworld.

It would be very interesting to know if there were a definite connection between the scene on the ash-chest and the dead whose ashes it contained. When the fish-tailed sea-god entangles a man to bear him off, does it mean drowning at sea? And when a man is caught in the writhing serpent-legs of the Medusa, or of the winged snake-power, does it mean a fall to earth; a death from the earth, in some manner; as a fall, or the dropping of a rock, or the bite of a snake? And the soul carried off by a winged centaur: is it a man dead of some passion that carried him away?

But more interesting even than the symbolic scenes are those scenes from actual life, such as boar-hunts, circus-games, processions, departures in covered wagons, ships sailing away, city gates being stormed, sacrifice being performed, girls with open scrolls, as if reading at school; many banquets with man and woman on the banqueting couch, and slaves playing music, and children around: then so many really tender farewell scenes, the dead saying good-bye to his wife, as he goes on the journey, or as the chariot bears him off, or the horse waits; then the soul alone, with the death-dealing spirits standing by with their hammers that gave the blow. It is as Dennis says, the breeze of Nature stirs one's soul. I asked the gentle old man if he knew anything about the urns. But no! no! He knew nothing at all. He had only just come. He counted for nothing. So he protested. He was one of those gentle, shy Italians too diffident even to look at the chests he was guarding. But when I told him what I thought some of the scenes meant he was fascinated like a child, full of wonder, almost breathless. And I thought again, how much more Etruscan than Roman the Italian of to-day is: sensitive, diffident, craving really for symbols and mysteries, able to be delighted with true delight over small things, violent in spasms, and altogether without sternness or natural will-to-power. The will-to-power is a secondary thing in an Italian, reflected on to him from the Germanic races that have almost engulfed him.

The boar-hunt is still a favourite Italian sport, the grandest sport of Italy. And the Etruscans must have loved it, for they represent it again and again, on the tombs. It is difficult to know what exactly the boar symbolized to them. He occupies often the centre of the scene, where the one who dies should be: and where the bull of sacrifice is. And often he is attacked, not by men, but by young winged boys, or by spirits. The dogs climb in the trees around him, the double axe is swinging to come down on him, he lifts up his tusks in a fierce wild pathos. The archaeologists say that it is Meleager and the boar of Calydon, or Hercules and the fierce brute of Erymanthus. But this is not enough. It is a symbolic scene: and it seems as if the boar were himself the victim this time, the wild, fierce fatherly life hunted down by dogs and adversaries. For it is obviously the boar who must die: he is not, like the lions and griffins, the attacker. He is the father of life running free in the forest, and he must die. They say too he represents winter: when the feasts for the dead were held. But on the very oldest archaic vases the lion and the boar are facing each other, again and again, in symbolic opposition.

Fascinating are the scenes of departures, journeyings in covered wagons drawn by two or more horses, accompanied by driver on foot and friend on horseback, and dogs, and met by other horsemen coming down the road. Under the arched tarpaulin tilt of the wagon reclines a man, or a woman, or a whole family: and all moves forward along the highway with wonderful slow surge. And the wagon, as far as I saw, is always drawn by horses, not by oxen.

This is surely the journey of the soul. It is said to represent even the funeral procession, the ash-chest being borne away to the cemetery, to be laid in the tomb. But the *memory* in the scene seems much deeper than that. It gives so strongly the feeling of a people

VOLTERRA

who have trekked in wagons, like the Boers, or the
Mormons, from one land to another.

They say these covered-wagon journeys are peculiar
to Volterra, found represented in no other Etruscan
places. Altogether the feeling of the Volterran scenes
is peculiar. There is a great sense of *journeying*: as
of a people which remembers its migrations, by sea
as well as land. And there is a curious restlessness,
unlike the dancing surety of southern Etruria; a touch
of the Gothic.

In the upstairs rooms there are many more ash-
chests, but mostly representing Greek subjects: so
called. Helen and the Dioscuri, Pelops, Minotaur,
Jason, Medea fleeing from Corinth, Oedipus and the
Sphinx, Ulysses and the Sirens, Eteocles and Polynices,
Centaurs and Lapithae, the Sacrifice of Iphigenia—
all are there, just recognizable. There are so many
Greek subjects that one archaeologist suggested that
these urns must have been made by a Greek colony
planted there in Volterra after the Roman conquest.

One might almost as well say that *Timon of Athens*
was written by a Greek colonist planted in England
after the overthrow of the Catholic Church. These
" Greek " ash-chests are about as Grecian as *Timon of
Athens* is. The Greeks would have done them so much
" better."

No, the " Greek " scenes are innumerable, but it
is only just recognizable what they mean. Whoever
carved these chests knew very little of the fables they

were handling : and fables they were, to the Etruscan
artificers of that day, as they would be to the Italians of
this. The story was just used as a peg upon which the
native Volterran hung his fancy, as the Elizabethans
used Greek stories for their poems. Perhaps also the
alabaster cutters were working from old models, or the
memory of them. Anyhow, the scenes show nothing
of Hellas.

Most curious these " classic " subjects : so un-
classic ! To me they hint at the Gothic which lay
unborn in the future, far more than at the Hellenistic
past of the Volterran Etruscan. For, of course, all
these alabaster urns are considered late in period, after
the fourth century B.C. The Christian sarcophagi of the
fifth century A.D. seem much more nearly kin to these
ash-chests of Volterra than do contemporary Roman
chests : as if Christianity really rose, in Italy, out of
Etruscan soil, rather than out of Graeco-Roman. And
the first glimmering of that early, glad sort of Christian
art, the free touch of Gothic within the classic, seems
evident in the Etruscan scenes. The Greek and Roman
" boiled " sort of form gives way to a raggedness of
edge and a certain wildness of light and shade which
promises the later Gothic, but which is still held down
by the heavy mysticism from the East.

Very early Volterran urns were probably plain stone
or terra-cotta. But no doubt Volterra was a city long
before the Etruscans penetrated into it, and probably
it never changed character profoundly. To the end,

the Volterrans burned their dead : there are practically
no long sarcophagi of Lucumones. And here most of
all one feels that the *people* of Volterra, or Velathri,
were not Oriental, not the same as those who made
most show at Tarquinii. This was surely another tribe,
wilder, cruder, and far less influenced by the old
Aegean influences. In Caere and Tarquinii the aborigines were deeply overlaid by incoming influences
from the East. Here not! Here the wild and un-
tamable Ligurian was neighbour, and perhaps kin, and
the town of wind and stone kept, and still keeps, its
northern quality.

So there the ash-chests are, an open book for anyone
to read who will, according to his own fancy. They
are not more than two feet long, or thereabouts, so
the figure on the lid is queer and stunted. The classic
Greek or Asiatic could not have borne that. It is a
sign of barbarism in itself. Here the northern spirit
was too strong for the Hellenic or Oriental or ancient
Mediterranean instinct. The Lucumo and his lady had
to submit to being stunted, in their death-effigy. The
head is nearly life-size. The body is squashed small.

But there it is, a portrait-effigy. Very often, the lid
and the chest don't seem to belong together at all. It
is suggested that the lid was made during the lifetime
of the subject, with an attempt at real portraiture :
while the chest was bought ready-made, and apart. It
may be so. Perhaps in Etruscan days there were the
alabaster workshops as there are to-day, only with

rows of ash-chests portraying all the vivid scenes we still can see: and perhaps you chose the one you wished your ashes to lie in. But more probably, the workshops were there, the carved ash-chests were there, but you did not select your own chest, since you did not know what death you would die. Probably you only had your portrait carved on the lid, and left the rest to the survivors.

So maybe, and most probably, the mourning relatives hurriedly *ordered* the lid with the portrait-bust, after the death of the near one, and then chose the most appropriate ash-chest. Be it as it may, the two parts are often oddly assorted: and so they were found with the ashes inside them.

But we must believe that the figure on the lid, grotesquely shortened, is an attempt at a portrait. There is none of the distinction of the southern Etruscan figures. The heads are given the " imperious " tilt of the Lucumones, but here it becomes almost grotesque. The dead nobleman may be wearing the necklace of office and holding the sacred patera or libation-dish in his hand; but he will not, in the southern way, be represented ritualistically as naked to below the navel; his shirt will come to his neck; and he may just as well be holding the tippling wine-cup in his hand as the sacred patera; he may even have a wine-jug in his other hand, in full carousal. Altogether the peculiar " sacredness," the inveterate symbolism of the southern Etruscans, is here gone. The religious power is broken.

It is very evident in the ladies : and so many of the figures are ladies. They are decked up in all their splendour, but the mystical formality is lacking. They hold in their hands wine-cups or fans or mirrors, pomegranates or perfume-boxes, or the queer little books which perhaps were the wax tablets for writing upon. They may even have the old sexual and death symbol of the pine-cone. But the *power* of the symbol has almost vanished. The Gothic actuality and idealism begins to supplant the profound *physical* religion of the southern Etruscans, the true ancient world.

In the museum there are jars and bits of bronze, and the pateras with the hollow knob in the middle. You may put your two middle fingers in the patera, and hold it ready to make the last libation of life, the first libation of death, in the correct Etruscan fashion. But you will not, as so many of the men on these ash-chests do, hold the symbolic dish upside down, with the two fingers thrust into the " mundus." The torch upside down means the flame has gone below, to the underworld. But the patera upside down is somehow shocking. One feels the Volterrans, or men of Velathri, were slack in the ancient mysteries.

At last the rain stopped crashing down icily in the silent inner courtyard ; at last there was a ray of sun. And we had seen all we could look at for one day. So we went out, to try to get warmed by a kinder heaven.

There are one or two tombs still open, especially two outside the Porta a Selci. But I believe, not having seen them, they are of small importance. Nearly all the tombs that have been opened in Volterra, their contents removed, have been filled in again, so as not to lose two yards of the precious cultivable land of the peasants. There were many tumuli: but most of them are levelled. And under some were curious round tombs built of unsquared stones, unlike anything in southern Etruria. But then, Volterra is altogether unlike southern Etruria.

One tomb has been removed bodily to the garden of the archaeological museum in Florence: at least its contents have. There it is built up again as it was when discovered in Volterra in 1861, and all the ash-chests are said to be replaced as they stood originally. It is called the Inghirami Tomb, from the famous Volterran archaeologist Inghirami.

A few steps lead down into the one circular chamber of the tomb, which is supported in the centre by a square pillar, apparently supposed to be left in the rock. On the low stone bed that encircles the tomb stand the ash-chests, a double row of them, in a great ring encircling the shadow.

The tomb belongs all to one family, and there must be sixty ash-chests, of alabaster, carved with the well-known scenes. So that if this tomb is really arranged as it was originally, and the ash-chests progress from the oldest to the latest counter-clockwise, as is said, one ought to be able to see certainly a century or two of development in the Volterran urns.

But one is filled with doubt and misgiving. Why, oh why, wasn't the tomb left intact as it was found, where it was found? The garden of the Florence museum is vastly instructive, if you want object-lessons about the Etruscans. But who wants object-lessons about vanished races? What one wants is a contact. The Etruscans are not a theory or a thesis. If they are anything, they are an *experience*.

And the experience is always spoilt. Museums, museums, museums, object-lessons rigged out to illustrate the unsound theories of archaeologists, crazy attempts to co-ordinate and get into a fixed order that which has no fixed order and will not be co-ordinated! It is sickening! Why must all experience be systematized? Why must even the vanished Etruscans be reduced to a system? They never will be. You break all the eggs, and produce an omelette which is neither Etruscan nor Roman nor Italic nor Hittite, nor anything else, but just a systematized mess. Why can't incompatible things be left incompatible? If you make an omelette out of a hen's egg, a plover's, and an ostrich's, you won't have a grand amalgam or unification of hen and plover and ostrich into something we may call " oviparity." You'll have that formless object, an omelette.

So it is here. If you try to make a grand amalgam of Cerveteri and Tarquinia, Vulci, Vetulonia, Volterra, Chiusi, Veii, then you won't get the essential *Etruscan* as a result, but a cooked-up mess which has no life-meaning at all. A museum is not a first-hand contact: it is an illustrated lecture. And what one wants is the actual vital touch. I don't want to be "instructed"; nor do many other people.

They could take the more homeless objects for the museums, and still leave those that *have* a place in their own place: the Inghirami Tomb here at Volterra.

But it is useless. We walk up the hill and out of the Florence gate, into the shelter under the walls of the huge mediaeval castle which is now a State prison. There is a promenade below the ponderous walls, and a scrap of sun, and shelter from the biting wind. A few citizens are promenading even now. And beyond, the bare green country rises up in waves and sharp points, but it is like looking at the choppy sea from the prow of a tall ship; here in Volterra we ride above all.

And behind us, in the bleak fortress, are the prisoners. There is a man, an old man now, who has written an opera inside those walls. He had a passion for the piano: and for thirty years his wife nagged him when he played. So one day he silently and suddenly killed her. So, the nagging of thirty years silenced, he got thirty years of prison, and *still* is not allowed to play the piano. It is curious.

There were also two men who escaped. Silently and secretly they carved marvellous likenesses of themselves out of the huge loaves of hard bread the prisoners get. Hair and all, they made their own effigies lifelike.

Then they laid them in the bed, so that when the warder's light flashed on them he should say to himself : " There they lie sleeping, the dogs ! "

And so they worked, and they got away. It cost the governor, who loved his houseful of malefactors, his job. He was kicked out. It is curious. He should have been rewarded, for having such clever children, sculptors in bread.